Guide's Greatest
MIRACLE STORIES

HELEN LEE, editor

Guide's Greatest
MIRACLE STORIES

REVIEW AND HERALD® PUBLISHING ASSOCIATION
HAGERSTOWN, MD 21740

The editor assumes full responsibility for the accuracy of all facts
and quotations as cited in this book.

This book was
Edited by Helen Lee
Designed by Kimberly Haupt
Cover designed by Brandon Reese
Cover art by Ralph Butler
Electronic makeup by Shirley M. Bolivar
Typeset: 13/16 Goudy

PRINTED IN U.S.A.

05 04 03 02 01   5 4 3 2 1

R&H Cataloging Service
Guide's greatest miracle stories,
     compiled and edited by Helen Lee

     1. Miracles—Stories.   I. Lee, Helen, 1976

          231.73

ISBN 0-8280-1575-9

A Special Thanks

Thanks and praise to our God for His unconditional love and for the miracles He works on our behalf.

A special thanks to Jeannette Johnson, Randy Fishell, Kelli Gauthier, Melissa Bowen, and the many others who were involved in the production of this book.

And to family and friends, words could never fully express how much I appreciate your prayers and support.

Contents

The Book That Would Not Burn

by Mrs. John F. Underhill

M other, Mother!" Tona called as she ran into the house. "There's a strange man kneeling behind the gooseberry bushes."

"Don't get so excited, Tona," her mother replied.

"But he might be one of those booksellers. They're selling religious books all over the neighborhood. Father said they wouldn't be welcome at our house, but the man's coming right up the path to our door! Mother, what should we do?"

"We'll let him in, of course. No true German woman ever turned a stranger away from the door."

Mother dried her hands on the kitchen towel and then went to the door to welcome the stranger. After a few words of greeting, she invited him into the parlor. Tona sat on a stool beside Mother's chair and listened to the Christian bookseller as he described his book.

"The book begins with the terrible persecutions of Christians during the time of the early church," he said. "Then there are stories about great Reformers. Some of them were from Germany."

Mother seemed very interested. "I studied about them in school," she said.

The man continued to explain the great controversy between Christ and Satan and how God's people would finally live on the new earth, where sin and sorrow would no longer exist.

"Oh, I want that book," said Mother, "but I am not very good at reading English. I went to school in Germany, and I never learned to read English very well."

"I can get this book for you in German if you wish," the man said with a smile.

Tona could see the longing in her mother's eyes. "Let's get it, Mother. We could save part of the egg money. Surely we would have the right amount by the time he comes to deliver it."

Mother thought for a moment. It seemed like a lot of money for just one book. Tona needed new shoes and many other things. And what would her husband Franz say? He was totally against religious things. But she did want to know more about the German Reformers and about the reward of the faithful.

"I'll give you the money I earned from picking

gooseberries," said Tona. "I have more than enough for the down payment." She went to her room and brought back her little jar of coins.

"I do not wish to take your money," objected Mother.

"Well, we can call it my book, and I'll help with the eggs. Please let's order the book in German."

Mother finally agreed, and the order was made out. Just before the colporteur left, he asked, "May I have prayer with you before I go?"

Mother was happy to grant his request. She had been raised in a Christian home, where prayers had been a part of the daily routine. But it had been a long time since anyone had prayed in her home. She and Tona knelt by their chairs and reverently bowed their heads.

The man offered a simple prayer, asking God's blessings on the home and on the book that had been ordered. Then Mother prayed in German, because that was more natural for her. She prayed that they would have enough money to pay for the book and that the book would be a great blessing in their humble home and in the little German settlement along the Missouri River.

When they rose from their knees, the man shook hands with Tona and Mother. "Thank you for your prayer. I don't understand the German language very well, but I'm sure the Lord does."

Then with a cheery goodbye, he went down the path toward the road, promising to return in three weeks with Tona's book.

The days passed quickly. In great anticipation of her new book, Tona faithfully gathered the eggs and put them in the big egg crate, ready to be sold. Mother sold some vegetables and added some of the money to the pile of coins in Tona's jar.

"We have more than enough for the book," said Tona as she counted the coins one day. "We even have enough for my new shoes."

Mother was glad and looked forward to reading the wonderful stories in her native language. She wondered whether Franz would read them too. He was a good reader, but he was definitely not interested in religion.

At last the day of delivery came. Tona saw the bookseller coming and wondered if he would kneel down to pray behind the gooseberry bushes as he had that first time. But he walked straight toward her. "I have a book for you, Tona."

"Oh, thank you," said Tona. "Now Mother can read those stories in German!"

That night after the dishes were done, Mother and Tona began reading the new book. They read about great men who were willing to die—even burn at the stake—for their faith.

One night Tona was reading the book by herself.

She found it hard to read German, since her lessons in school were mostly in English. She missed Mother's help, but Mother had gone to visit a sick neighbor. Father could read German too, but he was out doing the evening chores.

Tona stopped to take the bread out of the oven. She sniffed the air appreciatively and then returned to her book.

Several minutes later Father walked in with the milk. He washed his hands at the sink and smelled the warm, fresh bread.

"It looks and smells good," he remarked. Then he noticed what Tona was reading. "German?"

Tona nodded.

"A religious book?"

"Yes, Father. It's a very good book."

"Where did you get it, Tona?"

Tona was almost too afraid to answer. She didn't like the look on Father's face. But she decided to be brave like the Reformers and tell the truth no matter what.

"Mother and I bought it with egg money and with what I saved from picking gooseberries."

Father picked up the book, flipped through the pages, then slammed the cover down. "You bought it from a Christian bookseller, didn't you? The neighbors have been talking about those books. I will not have one of them in my house!"

He carried the book over to the wood-burning cookstove and lifted its lid.

"Please, Father, please don't burn my book!" Tona begged, running toward him and clutching his sleeve. "It is a good book. It is a message from God."

But Father pushed her aside and threw the book into the stove, on top of the red coals. He replaced the lid noisily and said, "There! Maybe that will put a stop to this religious nonsense." He put on his cap and went outside.

Tona was too stunned to say a word. After the door closed behind Father, she lifted the stove lid, hoping she might still rescue her treasured book. But it was too late. The beautiful covers were already being devoured by the hot, yellow flames. Tona crawled into bed and cried herself to sleep.

It was quite late when Mother returned from the neighbor's, so she didn't hear about what had happened until the following morning. As she started building a fire to make breakfast, she noticed the charred remains of something big that would not shake down. She removed it from the stove and brushed off the ashes. Tona walked into the kitchen just as Mother was wiping away the black char from the item's remains.

"My book!" exclaimed Tona. "It didn't all burn, did it?" She explained what had happened the night before.

"My poor Franz," Mother said. "I was hoping this book would help him, too. Maybe it still can." The fire had destroyed the covers, the preface, and the index, but the most important part was still readable.

Tona took the remains of the book to her room. From now on she would read it only when Father was gone. He would never know she still had it.

For many days Mother and Tona read the charred leaves of *The Great Controversy* while Father was in the field. They read the parallel scriptures from the Bible and knew it was the truth. They shared the experience with some of the neighbors, and they came to see the wonderful book God had protected from the fire.

One night while Franz was eating supper, he asked, "What happened to the book I tried to burn? Some of the neighbors have been talking about it."

"We still have it," said Mother. "Tona's been taking care of it."

"I would like to see it," Franz said. "Will you get it for me?"

"Will you destroy it, Father?" Tona asked timidly.

"No, Tona, I promise not to harm it. I want to see the book that a hot fire could not burn."

Tona went to her room and brought out the book. She handed it to her father, who took it hesitantly. He shook his head and said, "I don't understand why it didn't burn. The fire was hot that night—hot enough to bake bread."

"Do you think it was because the man prayed about it?" asked Tona. "Maybe God has something special for it to do."

"I think you're right," said Father. "Perhaps He has a message in it for me."

During the following winter the three of them read and reread the book. Not "from cover to cover," because there were no covers! But they read it from the first charred page to the last, comparing quoted scripture with the ones in Mother's German Bible.

The following spring a man came to follow up the work of the Christian bookseller who had sold *The Great Controversy*. He was surprised to find many people who believed the book's message about Jesus, including Tona and her father and mother. A church was soon established in the German settlement.

When the Christian bookseller knelt by the gooseberry bushes, little did he dream of the far-reaching results God would bring about through the sale of Tona's book, the book that would not burn.

2

The Flying Kite Prayer

by Josephine Cunnington Edwards

Abubaker held his mother's hand tightly as they fled from their village in India. It was World War II, and bombs were destroying homes all over the country. As they hurried along with the other villagers, little Abubaker and his mother were separated from his father.

"Where's Daddy?" Abubaker asked.

"I don't know, son," his mother answered. "It's wartime, and many people get lost or hurt. Maybe Daddy's been killed."

But Abubaker refused to believe that his father was dead. He remembered his father walking and talking with him, helping him fly kites, and playing little games.

Abubaker remembered their house down in the village and the store where his father used to sell cloth, soap, spices, saris, and teapots. It had been a wonderful shop. Abubaker used to sit on a pile of rugs and watch Daddy sell things for hours at a time and not get tired. He loved to smell the tea from Ceylon, the cloves from Zanzibar, the figs from Smyrna, and the dates from Egypt. Now it was all gone. Abubaker and his mother had been moved to a city in the hills, far away from the fighting.

One day as Abubaker walked by a school in the hills, he stopped to look inside. He saw children reading books and writing on slates. He watched for a long time. Just before noon they all knelt down and shut their eyes. The teacher began to talk to someone. Abubaker looked all around as quietly as he could, but he couldn't see anyone.

When all the boys were going home, Abubaker spoke to one of them. "Who were you talking to when you were kneeling down?"

The boy smiled. "Oh, we were talking to the great God, to Allah."

Abubaker trotted along beside the bigger boy and thought about this strange thing for a minute.

"Did he hear you?" he asked again.

"Of course," the older boy assured him. "We've learned from our missionary that God cares and answers us when we pray."

"Every time?" Abubaker persisted.

"Oh, yes, but not always right away, and not just

what we ask for. God gives us what's best for us. But here's where I have to turn. Come visit our school, and they will tell you more about these things." With that, the boy turned and headed for home.

Abubaker walked slowly toward the place where he and his mother lived. *I'm sure it's best for us to have Daddy*, he thought. *And if God hears those boys, I think he might hear me.*

He walked along, wondering how he could pray. As he passed a little shop, Abubaker had a bright idea. The shop had hardly anything for sale, but there were some beautiful kites made of bright colored paper. Abubaker bought the biggest kite he could buy with his coins. Then he went home with his treasure.

His mother wasn't home, so he took the kite inside, got the writing instruments, and started writing a prayer on the big kite. Surely God—if He were up there on the other side of the clouds—would see the kite bobbing. He would likely lean over and read the prayer he had written on it.

Abubaker told God who he was and where he had lived and where he was now and how badly he wanted to see his daddy. Then he went out in the hills to fly his kite. He used up all his string so that the kite could get as close to the clouds as possible. He wanted it to be easy for God to read his message. He didn't know much about God, but he was doing the best he knew to do.

Suddenly a big gust of wind broke the string. The kite flopped around in the air and then went down. Abubaker walked home slowly, hoping the great God had had time to read the request.

Abubaker didn't know this, but the kite tumbled down on top of a railroad train that was winding through the hills on the way to the coast. There it lay, flapping around with the string caught on some bars on the back of a car. And there it rode and fluttered all the way to Calcutta.

Meanwhile, Abubaker's father was in Calcutta, longing to find his wife and son. He met every train he could, hoping to see his loved ones.

This day the train from the hills thundered into the station. Abubaker's father watched everyone get off, but his wife and son weren't on the train. Then he saw a kite dangling along the side. *Little Abubaker loves these,* he thought as he reached up and grabbed the broken kite.

He saw the boyish writing and started to read. "Dear God, I am Abubaker. I want to find my daddy. I think you can see me here, God. I'm at the hill village flying a kite here in the field. I know we—"

But Abubaker's father didn't wait to read the rest. He ran as fast as he could to catch a train into the hill country. He knew exactly where to find little Abubaker and his mother.

3

God Struck the Organ Dumb

by Norma B. Youngberg

Francis Pohan sat on the organ stool in the front room of his home in Borneo. Looking at a songbook, he played the notes of a hymn with his right hand, then with his left hand. He was determined to master the song. But when he put both hands on the keys and tried to play, the melody just didn't sound right.

"What's the matter with me today?" he said to himself. "My fingers are like lumps of mud."

He got up from the organ and went outside where his sister, Ellen, was sitting under the big durian tree, reading one of her books.

She looked up at him and asked, "Isn't this your practice time?"

"Yes, but I can't seem to hit the keys right," he replied, "so I thought I'd come out and look for the little truck I lost yesterday."

As he hunted for his toy in the long grass, Francis thought about how they had gotten the organ. Not many people had one. And certainly missionary families on the island of Borneo in Sarawak did not usually have such an instrument.

"If we could only have an organ of our own," Francis had often said to Ellen, "it would be like heaven."

"Perhaps you should pray about it," their father had suggested. "Maybe God will help us get one."

When they finally got an organ, they knew it was in answer to the prayers they had offered. A man was moving away from the country and he asked such a low price for his organ that the Pohans decided to buy it.

"I should go back and try that hymn again," Francis said to himself, "but I know I can't play it."

At that moment the boy heard some cars go by on the jungle road. Then he saw soldiers in uniform coming along the path. It was wartime in Borneo, and enemy soldiers sometimes made trips out into the country around Kuching, foraging for food and other things they wanted.

Francis' heart beat fast as the soldiers came up to the house. There were about a dozen of them. They laughed and looked friendly enough and spoke to the children in loud voices.

"Is your father home? Is he in the house?"

Father must have heard the noise because he came out the front door and stood before the enemy soldiers.

"What do you want of me?" he asked them.

"We are from the school," their leader explained. Francis remembered that the soldiers had taken over the big Mission Training School near the town of Kuching. They were using it to train soldiers.

"We are looking for an organ or a piano. We need some kind of musical instrument in our school." The leader looked at Father. "Is there an organ in your chapel here?"

Father shook his head. "We did have one, but some of your people took it quite a while ago."

"Do you have one in your house?" one of the soldiers asked.

"We have one," Father admitted.

Francis looked at Ellen. Her face was pale. He could see that she was holding back tears with great effort. He wanted to tell the soldiers that the organ was theirs, that God had answered their prayers and given it to them. Instead he stood quietly in the grass and scuffed a twig with his bare toe.

He knew that when enemy soldiers asked for something, they weren't just asking for it. They were demanding it, and it had to be given to them. Whatever the soldiers wanted, they took.

Father was already leading the soldiers into the

house. Francis hurried in with them and stood watching as the leader looked the organ over.

"Does it work?" he asked. "Is it in good order?"

"Yes, I think so," Father answered in a low voice.

"Better try it," the leader ordered one of the soldiers.

The young officer sat down. He pumped the pedals and pressed the keys, but no sound came out of the organ. He looked up at the leader and then tried again. His face turned red.

"It doesn't work, sir," he said.

Another soldier sat down and tried to play the organ, but it was still silent. Not a sound came out of it.

Francis was frightened, but he had been praying ever since the soldiers came into the yard and asked about the organ. He prayed, "Dear God, please don't let them take away the organ you gave us."

Now the leader turned to Father. "The instrument seems to be out of order." His face was red and angry.

Father's voice was a little unsteady. "It usually plays very well. There must be some small thing wrong. I'm sure it can be easily fixed."

"Do you know of anyone in this place who could repair it?" the leader asked his men. Then he turned to Father and asked him the same question. None of them knew of anyone.

The leader was getting impatient. He handed his

gun to one of the other men and sat down at the organ himself. He pressed the keys. He looked at the pedals and pumped them hard. He examined the swells and even shook the organ. It was all of no use. Not a sound came out.

The officer stood up, reached for his gun, and said in disgust, "Your organ is no good—positively useless! We couldn't use a piece of junk like that!" With some insulting words he called his soldiers after him and they went out the door and down the path to the road.

The whole Pohan family stood on the porch and watched them go. When they had disappeared in the trees a little way down the path, Francis hurried to the organ. He pedaled. He played on the keys, but no sound came out. The organ was silent. Something was certainly wrong with it. A big lump appeared in his throat.

Father and Mother looked at the organ. "I can't understand what can be wrong with it," Father said. "It's of no use to us either. Just the same, I'm glad the soldiers didn't take it. Surely it can be fixed."

He went back to his work, and Francis went outside where Ellen had returned to her book. For a half hour the two children sat looking at pictures and talking about the soldiers. Both of them felt very sad about the organ.

"I'm going in," Francis finally said. "I'll get Father's tools and take the organ to pieces. I'm going to find out why it won't work. Maybe the white ants have eaten a hole in the bellows."

He went back into the house and looked at the organ. "I'll try it once more," he told himself as he put the hammer on the floor.

He sat on the stool and pushed the pedals. When he played the keys, the music came out as usual.

"Mother, Father, Ellen!" Francis yelled. "The organ is all right. It isn't hurt at all! It plays as well as ever!"

Father and Mother hurried into the room. Ellen came running and burst in the door, her eyes shining.

"Who was praying about this?" Father asked.

"I was," everyone answered at once.

"It is God who struck the organ dumb," Father told them.

"It must have been God's angel who troubled me, so I left the organ during my usual practice time," Francis spoke in an awed whisper.

"It must have been," Ellen said. "If you had kept on playing, the soldiers would have heard you as they came up the path."

"And even after they went—right after—it still didn't—"

Father smiled in a solemn way. "Of course it didn't because the soldiers were still close enough to hear. God's angels always manage everything perfectly."

In that moment the whole family felt the unseen presence of the One who was a living messenger from heaven. The veil between heaven and earth was parted just a little, and they knelt in reverent thankfulness around the organ that God had struck dumb.

4

Abel and the Viper

by Reinhold Klingbeil
as told by Albertina Klingbeil Tilstra

A bel and a few others set out on an expedition in West New Guinea, a land of large plains, hidden valleys, and towering mountains. They often walked when visiting different villages because even jeeps had to be left behind when the hills were too steep or the jungle too thick.

Masses of tangled vines made progress difficult, but the men trudged on. Three or four boys walked ahead, loaded with bundles and boxes—the supplies for the journey. Elder Vijsma (pronounced Vaismah) followed them the best he could, and Abel brought up the rear.

Suddenly a terrified scream pierced the jungle. Elder Vijsma rushed to Abel's side to find him clutching his foot. It had been bitten by a vicious adder or viper, probably the death adder, which is very poisonous.

Poor Abel fell to the ground, moaning in pain. The burden bearers who had been walking ahead came back quickly at the sound of the screaming. They gathered around Elder Vijsma and the stricken Papuan helper.

What could they do? The group had no medicines, except a small quantity of permanganate crystals. They were helpful for disinfecting vegetables, but of what use were they for snake bites?

Elder Vijsma put a makeshift tourniquet around Abel's leg a little above the bite. Cutting the skin, he put some permanganate crystals into the bleeding incision.

The pain grew worse, and the foot swelled alarmingly. To make matters worse, the sun was beginning to set. Soon it would be dark.

Elder Vijsma found a stream nearby and carried water to the patient. Using Abel's shirt, he applied cold compresses to the swelling foot. He could do no more. Or could he?

He knelt by Abel's side and prayed. After he arose from his knees, he continued to give cold compresses, the best treatment available in the jungle. The pain increased, and even the leg began to swell.

Again Elder Vijsma prayed. Fervently he asked God to save Abel's life. He also asked God for a sign that he might know that his prayer would be answered.

Elder Vijsma opened his eyes, and as he looked at

one of the nearby bushes, he saw a very bright light. He knew that there was no light in the wilderness at night, and certainly no native could make such a bright light! A feeling of awe came over him. It must have been like the feeling Moses had when he saw the burning bush. In amazement and deep thankfulness he accepted the miraculous light as an immediate answer from God.

But Elder Vijsma and his helpers saw much more than the bright light. They saw Abel—who only moments before had been lying on the ground groaning in pain and in danger of immediate death—sit up. After a few more cold compresses, he stood up and said, "I'm all right. There is no more pain. Let us continue our trip."

The next morning they arrived at Manokwari and went to the small government hospital, where a doctor examined Abel's foot.

"But there is no trace of a snake bite," the doctor said.

Not only had God healed Abel of the deadly effects of the viper's bite, but He had even removed the marks of its fangs. Yes, God still answers prayer.

5

Who Opened the Prison Door?

by Inez Brasier

Hadewyck smiled as she hurried home along the cleanest street of the cleanest town in Holland. "Jesus will make our hearts as clean as our town," she whispered to her friend Elizabeth. "I wish all our neighbors would learn to love Him as we do!"

But in the town of Leeuwarden 400 years ago there weren't many people who loved Jesus. In fact, most of them scowled at Christians and would not listen when Hadewyck and her friend tried to tell them of His great love.

One day rough soldiers arrested Hadewyck. They grabbed her arms so tightly that they hurt. "Help me, Jesus," she prayed as the cruel men rushed her along the street to the jail.

"We'll see if you'll keep talking about your

Jesus," the jailer said. "I vow you'll stop when you feel the thumbscrews!"

The key clicked in the lock, and Hadewyck was all alone in the prison cell. "Thank You, Jesus," she prayed. "Thank You that they did not kill me."

Sounds from the streets seeped through the keyhole, and Hadewyck counted the days by those noises. She knew when the heavy carts of wheat and corn were being hauled to the weigh bridge. She knew from the noise of the cattle when they were being driven to the market. And often she prayed.

One day as she was praying, a voice called her name. "Hadewyck!"

She looked around. There was no one in the room. Hadewyck kept praying, happy that no one could keep her from talking with Jesus.

"Hadewyck!" There was the voice again!

She looked at the door. It was shut, and there was no one in the room. She closed her eyes to talk to Jesus some more.

"Hadewyck! You must leave here!"

There had been no click of the key in the lock, but the door was open!

Hadewyck quickly drew her cloak around her shoulders and stepped into the street. But which way should she go? Where could she hide before anyone saw her?

She stepped into a large church near the jail and

walked up and down the aisles with the crowds of other people who were walking there. Then she heard the town drummer calling in the street, and her face turned pale.

"A female heretic has escaped!" the drummer shouted.

"The town gates have been shut," the excited crowd whispered. "She'll soon be caught!"

"She'll feel the thumbscrews!" said a passerby on the street.

"But how did she get out? She must be a witch to have opened that door!" said the jailer.

Hadewyck was sure from all the talk that she would soon be found in the church. She quietly slipped out.

The town drummer was going past. "A hundred guilders to the man who finds the heretic!" he shouted. "One hundred fifty guilders fine if anyone hides her!"

Surely now someone who knew her would see her and claim the 100 guilders! Where could she go? "Jesus, show me where to hide!"

The priests' tall house stood beside the church. Hadewyck remembered that the maid who worked there was her friend. She stepped inside. No one heard her as she climbed the stairs. No one heard her as she opened the attic door and closed it softly behind her.

She peeped through the window and saw soldiers rushing about. She quickly stepped away from the window, afraid that someone might look up and see her. She leaned against a chest to think.

"Thank You, Jesus, for keeping me safe so far," she prayed. "Show me what to do next."

A sound drifted through the attic door. "Maybe my friend is coming. I will listen for her."

After a while she heard the girl cleaning the hall below. Hadewyck slowly went down the attic steps, stopping often to listen.

"Little one," she whispered. "Little one!"

The girl looked up and smiled. Hadewyck had always been so good to her.

"Listen carefully, little one. I want you to go to my sister's home. Please tell her husband to bring a boat to the back of this house for me tonight."

The girl nodded and scurried down the stairs. Hadewyck heard the slam of a door and listened to the quick steps as they grew fainter.

The afternoon went by. At last it was dark outside, and the streets were quiet. Hadewyck crept down the stairs so carefully that her feet scarcely touched the steps. She walked lightly along the hall to the door that opened on the canal.

Her sister's husband was waiting in the boat. He reached up his hand to help her to a seat. Dipping his oars without a sound, he rowed to a place of safety.

"Jesus opened the prison door for me as He did for Peter," Hadewyck told him. "He kept people from recognizing me in the church, and He kept me safe in the priests' house until you came. I do thank Him tonight."

For many years Hadewyck told people about Jesus' love, and Jesus always kept her from harm. She lived until she was an old woman, and then she went peacefully to her rest.

6

The Lamp That Kept on Burning

by Phyllis Somerville

Please come and preach to us," pleaded a man who lived on an island off the coast of Korea.

The colporteur looked down, shifted his feet uneasily, and finally stammered, "I've never spoken in public before. You might be disappointed. I'm sure you can find a better speaker."

"There might be other speakers," the man replied, "but it may be a long time before one of them can come to our island. I've heard some of your beliefs, and I want to learn more. I'll also invite some of my friends to attend. Surely, you will not disappoint me."

The colporteur finally agreed, thinking that the man would bring his wife and maybe a friend or two. But what if more people came to the meeting? He very well knew how eager the Koreans were to hear the Gospel, and he knew that this was his God-given opportunity to speak for his Master.

"We will be looking for you," the man said as they parted.

Wondering why he had agreed, the colporteur made his way home to tell his wife. Together they knelt in earnest prayer. After getting up from their knees, they discussed what would be a good message and decided to use Daniel 2. "Many of our ministers seem to use it first," the colporteur reasoned.

"You'd better make some notes," his wife suggested.

"Notes!" he exclaimed. "I'd better write out the entire sermon word for word. I'm sure to forget some of it."

Together they sorted out the texts they needed. Knowing that the Lord was helping them think of the right words to say, the colporteur began to feel more confident.

The evening for the meeting arrived quickly—too quickly! But the colporteur knew his message well.

"Let's pray before we leave for the hall," he suggested to his wife. So again they knelt to ask God's blessing upon the little service.

They started early, well armed with equipment—Bible, sermon, and hymnal. As they walked down the dusty road, the colporteur and his wife kept overtaking small groups of people headed in the same direction. They paid little heed at first, thinking that there was some entertainment in the village.

However, as they got closer to the appointed place, the colporteur began to get cold sweat on his hands as it dawned on him that he was not going to speak to "one or two friends." All these people were coming to the meeting to listen to him!

They entered the shabby hall and looked at the audience of 150 eager people, packed into all the available space. The colporteur felt like a schoolboy wanting to run away and hide.

His wife noted his anxiety and whispered, "I'll be praying for you, dear."

Appreciating the encouragement, he added, "I'll need it. But God be praised for bringing out the folks to hear this humble servant."

The "publicity man" ambled up to them. "See, I brought my friends."

"It's wonderful that you have invited so many people, but I am not a public speaker," the colporteur said. "Do you think they will listen?"

"Yes, yes. They are all eager to hear about Jesus."

The colporteur quickly chose some hymns that he thought he could teach the crowd to sing, and prayerfully he went to the front of the hall. He noticed that there was only a little dish lamp on the table at the front of the room. The lamp was like those used in Bible times, a type still commonly used in some parts of the world.

The people did their best to learn the hymns he

taught them, and after a heartwarming prayer he proceeded to read his message. There was rapt attention and much nodding of heads.

But as their interest rose, the lamp grew dim. Too dim, in fact, for the colporteur to read his notes. He stopped abruptly and asked the man who had arranged the meeting whether more oil could be provided.

The embarrassed man stood up and humbly apologized to the colporteur. "We tried to buy more oil, but we couldn't. There won't be any more until a boat comes in, and that may take several days. I'm sorry, but we had already made arrangements and invited the folks. What should we do?"

The colporteur suddenly thought of the miracles in the Bible. There were even a couple in there about oil that didn't run out. "Let's pray," he announced.

It seems that all the heads were reverently bowed except one. The little fellow it belonged to was sitting on the front row. Maybe he was waiting to see what God would do, now that the man of God was asking for a miracle.

Suddenly he shouted, "Look at the lamp!"

The colporteur said a hasty amen and opened his eyes. "Praise God!" he shouted.

The lamp had flared up and was burning brightly! The room was in a hubbub. No one had ever seen anything like this before! The lamp continued to burn brightly on just one drop of oil. The audience insisted that the man resume his talk. Surely the God this man talked about was a God to be worshiped!

The colporteur felt as if he were living on a cloud. Assured of God's presence, he forgot his bashfulness and finished the sermon with power. The folks clamored for the meetings to continue, and so the encouraged speaker willingly and thankfully accepted the invitation. He knew God would work mightily.

The colporteur spoke for three more nights. Prayer was offered each night that God would perform a miracle because it was true that no oil could be purchased in the town. And during the seven hours of meetings the lamp continued to shine.

The light of the Gospel banished the darkness from the hearts of many people who had known nothing but idol worship. At the end of the meetings 60 people asked to be baptized. When a church was organized, its members declared that it was "the church where the light of truth will never go out."

7

Frozen Prayers

by Ron Graybill

Something strange was happening under the hood of the old truck that Friday morning. Mrs. Martin became tense when she noticed a wisp of white steam. Her fists tightened, and she forgot about the cold as she sat with her eyes glued on the hood. She hoped Jeff hadn't seen it.

Pushing her numb hands deeper into her overcoat pocket, she wondered what the steam was from. Had the water started to boil again? Would they be left stranded? She slowly relaxed, and the cold crept back in around her. It had been even colder than this the night before, colder than she or Jeff had anticipated.

"I'd like to get a ride with you to Mantica tomorrow," Mrs. Martin had said to him the day before.

Jeff had glanced down at the boards in the porch

for a moment, then had looked up with a quick scowl. "I can't wait for you. It's likely to be pretty cold here. My engine might freeze if I wait."

Jeff worked as a vegetable peddler and brought supplies to the isolated mining camps and ranches of the California gold country. The people who lived in the hills depended on him as their only contact with civilization. A radiator, cracked by a freeze, could mean disaster.

Realizing this, Mrs. Martin replied, "You could stay up the road a little way—close to the creek. Would it freeze there?"

Jeff paused a moment. "I guess I could, and I wouldn't have to drain my radiator either. I usually stay over by Sheep Ranch in a more protected spot, but why do you need to get to Mantica?"

"Well," Mrs. Martin replied, "I want to attend some Week of Prayer meetings. There's no church around here close enough for me to go to, so I want to meet with the folks down there and attend their meetings."

"I don't know much about prayer meetings, but I guess I can take you down in the morning."

"Thank you. I'll have breakfast ready when you come."

Cold wasn't the word for it. Little boys cracked the ice in the puddles on the way to school the next morning. And besides freezing puddles, the cold temperature had frozen the water inside the radiator of

Jeff's old truck. The ice had expanded and cracked the radiator.

This meant that when Jeff started the truck in the morning, the engine would begin to warm up and melt the ice. As the ice melted, the water would run out through the crack. The little bit of water that remained behind would get hot enough to boil and could boil away completely in a few minutes. More water would have to be added immediately. If it wasn't, there would be nothing to cool the engine. The engine would get hotter and hotter until it would begin to melt. As soon as that happened, the engine would stop and no one would ever be able to get it going again.

Jeff's old truck was boiling like a steam locomotive by the time he covered the short distance from where he had parked the truck overnight to Mrs. Martin's house. He brought it to a jerking halt in the yard. Throwing open the door, he jumped out, threw up the hood, twisted off the radiator cap, and released a geyser of white steam into the chilled morning air.

"Hurry up and bring me a bucket of water! My radiator's been ruined by the freeze last night."

Mrs. Martin came with the bucket and stood by quietly. Jeff began to pour in a small steady stream. But as some of the water trickled onto the frozen ground, Mrs. Martin felt all her hopes of attending the meeting drain away.

Jeff said nothing as he followed Mrs. Martin into

her house, where she had prepared breakfast for him. After eating in silence, Jeff repeated the process of filling the radiator. He emptied the bucket again and then slammed the hood. He gave the curt command, "Get in," thinking to himself, *She might as well come along. She caused the trouble, so she can share in the worry of making the trip too—if we make it.*

His disgust turned to a quiet desperation as he closed the door and backed out of the driveway. Somehow he had to make it to San Andreas, where he could get the truck repaired. Somehow he had to get the truck over the twisting narrow roads that led across the three mountain ranges that lay between here and the first little town, Sheep Ranch.

Houses were few, with only two camps before Sheep Ranch. Towns were even fewer—if you could call those wide spots in the road towns. He had to deliver goods at the mining camps and ranches because the people needed them—they were waiting.

At last there was one more creek, after which would be miles of deserted mountain country. After climbing another steep hill, Jeff brought the truck down to the rickety wooden bridge that spanned the last available water. He stopped just after crossing the bridge and made a quick descent to the edge of the creek. He filled the bucket with icy water, then came back up to fill the radiator for the last time. There would be no more water until just this side of Sheep Ranch.

When Jeff climbed back into the truck, Mrs. Martin noticed a snowflake on his sleeve and another on his battered hat. Soon there were many falling through the cold morning air.

Mrs. Martin watched the windshield wipers struggling with the snow that stuck to the windshield. She began to pray. "Dear God, it's my fault, and there's no more water now. Please fix the engine." Her cold lips formed the words slowly as she went on. "Help Jeff to sell all his goods so he will feel repaid for his trip. Lord, I want so much to attend those meetings and see some folks who believe as I do. Help us. Amen."

The red dirt on the banks beside the road soon turned white as snow continued to sift down through the gray morning onto the pines, firs, and manzanitas. The truck droned on, the only interruptions to the whir of the engine being the creaking and squeaking of the vehicle's frozen joints as it struck the rough spots on the road.

At the Shaw Mine, Jeff stopped just long enough to sell a few supplies, then moved on toward Sheep Ranch. He seemed to have forgotten that he had intended to get water at the mine, although he did mutter something about the strange fact that the engine didn't seem to boil any more. At Sheep Ranch, Jeff again left Mrs. Martin shivering in the truck as he went about his business there.

The next few miles of road were covered with a

muddy slush instead of pavement, and the truck's pace slowed to a crawl. Returning to the cab after a sale at a ranch house, Jeff again commented on the fact that the truck didn't need any water. He kept repeating, "That's funny; it doesn't boil anymore."

After driving off the main road to visit an isolated house, he made another strange observation. "I'm selling out of everything. I don't have any bread or butter left." Mrs. Martin kept silent about her prayer. She hardly expected Jeff to understand.

They slipped on through the morning. The snow let up now and then, but it was still bitterly cold in the truck. As they entered the last 10 miles of road before reaching San Andreas, they sped up a little as pavement again smoothed the way for them.

"There's a garage in San Andreas. We'll be able to check the water there." Jeff's voice cracked the silence of the moment.

Then something else startled Mrs. Martin—that wisp of steam! Again Jeff failed to notice. The tenseness returned to Mrs. Martin, but Jeff drove on unmindfully through the falling snow. At last they came to the curve that led into the narrow main street of San Andreas.

Pulling into a garage Jeff said to the attendant, "I'd better have you check the water."

The attendant went mechanically about his work—raised the hood, removed the cap, peered in, replaced the cap, closed the hood, then came back to the driver.

"It doesn't need any water, sir," he said. The crack in the radiator had disappeared.

8

Angel on the Trail

by Elizabeth Buhler Cott as told to Vinnie Ruffo

All night Joseph, the witch doctor, sent his eerie chants crashing through the jungle. "Ah-eeeeeee, ah-eeeee, ah-eeeee, ah-booommm, ah-booomm."

Inside our two-room house deep in the heart of the jungles of South America, chills were running up and down my spine. Alfred, my husband, and Joyce, our little girl, stirred in their beds. I knew that they too could not sleep. How could we ignore the creepy cries of Joseph, the devil worshiper? He always became very angry whenever we treated the sick Indians who came to our mission station.

"Alfred," I whispered in the dark, "what do you suppose he is up to now?"

My husband sighed and turned in bed. "Quiet, dear. Try to get some sleep."

Sleep? It was like listening to the devil's midnight carnival. I couldn't wait until the morning sun poured through the trees to chase the creeps away. Night in and night out Joseph filled our hearts with dread.

One morning whoops of excitement filled the air, and Indians came running toward our mission house. Two of them came quite close. We hurried outside, then gasped when we saw that they were Luti and Leo, the two men who assisted Joseph in his witchcraft. They waved a pistol and some guns in our faces. On the ground they had placed a dictaphone.

"Luti, Leo, where did you get those things?" my husband asked.

Then came the awful story.

A look of horror and anguish came over my husband's face. He asked, "But why? Why did you kill him?"

Luti whirled and showed his black teeth. "Him not have enough barter to pay us for carrying packs on trail."

We shivered at the attitude of these men. And we prayed, "O God, help us to make Christians out of these heathens." It seemed impossible at the moment, but we believed that God could do anything.

Shortly after this terrible happening, our family left the mission station on a Friday afternoon and walked along the trail that led to civilization. We wanted to find a secluded spot where we could worship God at sundown. We walked about a mile down the trail and stopped in a little clearing in the jungle. As we talked to God about our troubles, the fiery rays of the setting sun painted a flaming rash across the sky.

All at once it was dark! We realized that in the tropics nighttime does not come gradually. It comes fast. And now we had let darkness come upon us without being ready for it.

"How are we going to get back?" Joyce asked. "There isn't even a star in the sky." She sounded scared.

All around us came the buzzing and droning of countless insects. We knew, too, that there were wild animals that attacked at night. And snakes always filled us with horror, day or night.

My husband reached for my hand and Joyce's and pulled us close. "We didn't even remember to bring a lantern! Let's stay together and try to feel our way back."

The three of us crept along, trying to stay on a trail we couldn't see. The blackness was as thick as tar. We turned to the right and to the left, hitting bushes and trees and getting nowhere. The cry of a baboon startled us. The night noises suddenly began to form a jungle orchestra. For what seemed like hours we batted around in the dark.

Finally we admitted that we were lost. Lost in the

jungle! We crouched in the darkness, whispering to one another. Joyce said, "Daddy, Mommy—remember the verse in the Bible that says 'The angel of the Lord encampeth round about them that fear him, and delivereth them'?"

"Yes, Joyce," I whispered, thankful for the promise.

"Let's pray," she urged.

Dropping to our knees, we asked God to protect us from the dangers of the dark thick jungle. All at once my husband remembered that somewhere in his pockets he should have a box of matches. He fumbled around, and sure enough, he found them.

"We need some tall grass for a torch," he whispered. We reached around in the darkness until we found some. Soon we had enough light to find the narrow trail.

Gratefully holding our grass torch, we moved slowly and cautiously ahead. In the distance I saw a flame moving. Two men were out walking! I thought my heart would pop right out of my mouth. A little cry escaped my lips. I knew who those men were!

"Look," I cried. "There are Luti and Leo!" Luti was leading and carrying a large firebrand.

"They must be on the warpath," my husband replied. He tightened his hand on mine.

Who was to be their next victim? Both of us put an arm around Joyce and called on God for protection. We increased our pace, and at last in the distance we spotted our house. We ran the last few yards and stumbled inside. Our fear now turned to relief and gratitude to God for seeing us through.

But we had hardly entered when a sharp rap shook our door. A new wave of fear came over me. Suddenly the door swung open, and Luti stood before us. There was something else on his face besides the horrible war paint. There was a look of terror. We noticed that he was trembling.

"What is it, Luti?" snapped my husband. "Why do you come here?"

The painted Indian gasped only two words, *"Kenaima! Kenaima!"* (Kenaima means "enemy.")

"An enemy?" the three of us echoed.

"Who is the *kenaima?*" my husband asked. "Where did he go?"

Luti pointed in the direction of the trail. "Him make big fire. Him come in house. We must find him."

He pushed past all of us and began searching our two-room house. He crept under our springless cowhide bed while Leo poked and probed under our camp table and behind our folding organ. The two men searched through boxes and clothes, until every inch of our house had been combed. We watched in great amazement. We dared not try to stop them.

At last Luti spoke breathlessly, "No me got." With that he went outside looking for the intruder. In the meantime Joyce and I, in our bedroom, had dropped to our knees in prayer. I sensed that we were in great danger. These Indians were much too aroused over the little fire we had lighted on the trail and over this so-called *kenaima*. We felt very uncomfortable.

Luti entered the house again. My husband went to him quietly and placed an arm on his shoulder to calm him. "Did you see the *kenaima?*"

Luti pointed to the glowing fire on his firebrand. "Him big white man. We see big fire and four people. Papa Cott, Mamma Cott, child, and big white man."

A look of amazement came over my husband's face. "Big white man?" he repeated.

"Yes, all dressed in white. Man was guarding you and your family. He walked on trail with you. He come inside house with you."

I looked at my husband, and he looked at me. We were both thinking the same thing, and we felt very humble. Luti had seen our guardian angel.

"Luti," my husband spoke reverently, "the big white man you saw was not *kenaima*. He was our guardian angel. God sent him to protect us on the trail."

Luti's mouth fell open.

My husband told Luti and Leo that we were going to kneel in prayer and thank God for sending our guardian angel to protect us when we were in danger. "Will you kneel with us?" he invited them.

The two men knelt just as we did. Three missionaries and two devil worshipers smeared with war paint must have made a strange sight in that prayer session. Luti and Leo heard our little girl give thanks to God for keeping His promise, "The angel of the Lord encampeth round about those that fear him, and delivereth them."

After this experience a marvelous thing happened. Luti and Leo, no longer our heathen enemies, became our Christian friends. Instead of giving us trouble, they helped us many times.

9

The Dollars Kept Coming!

by Emerson Hartman

April 10, 1966, was the last day on which Mrs. Wright could pay the second half of her taxes before they would become delinquent. Her problem was that for two years she had been unable to pay. The city government would soon sell her home for those back taxes.

A frown crossed her usually peaceful face as she recounted her pitifully inadequate funds. Even before she paid tithe, there was far less than enough. Should she use her tithe money to help pay the bill?

Instantly putting away that thought, she counted out God's portion and tucked it into a tithe envelope. After all, if the city authorities sold her home, God would surely have something else for her.

She put the tax bill and her thin billfold into her purse and left the house. Instead of going at once to the courthouse, she drove to the house of Irma Johnson, a fellow deaconess and her best friend, who instantly saw that something was wrong.

"Edith! You look as though you've lost your best friend. What's the matter?"

"I feel as if the four walls of my house are falling in on me. It's my unpaid taxes."

"Taxes!" Mrs. Johnson exclaimed. "What's wrong with them?"

"Today's the last day to pay them, or they'll sell my home. And I just don't have the money to—"

"Let's get down on our knees and pray about it," her friend interrupted.

Down on their knees the two women went. Mrs. Wright was too depressed to pray much. Her church sister also said a short prayer. When they stood up, Mrs. Johnson told her, "Now go on and take care of your business, and stop worrying."

Mrs. Wright felt as if a ton had suddenly been lifted from her. Tears forced themselves from her eyes.

But even as she drove to the distant courthouse, worried thoughts kept returning. True, she knew the Lord would do His part. But how? And where would she live if the house was sold? Maybe she should keep the money to rent another house. No, that wouldn't be fair. Didn't the Bible say, "Render to Caesar the things that are Caesar's"? She needed to pay all she could.

When she reached the courthouse, the problem was still unsolved. She went to the cashier's window and asked the cashier for advice.

The cashier told her, "Pay your second installment. When you do that, all the overdue taxes become a bill to be paid, but the authorities can't touch your home. You must pay eventually, of course, but you can take as long as you need to."

"Then they can't sell my home?" Mrs. Wright cried eagerly.

"No, not after you pay the half that is due today."

This was a real break. "Then I'll pay it now. I have just enough in my purse."

Mrs. Wright handed the clerk her money. The clerk counted out the correct amount and handed back some change in one-dollar bills. Mrs. Wright slipped these in beside a thin sheaf of dollar bills she still had. Then she turned and crossed the hall to the delinquent-taxes window.

"May I make a small payment on my delinquent taxes?" she asked.

"Have you paid the bill?" the clerk asked, noting the tax bill Mrs. Wright was still holding in her hand.

"Yes. See, it is receipted. I had a few dollars left over, and the clerk said I could pay the delinquent taxes a little at a time."

"Yes, that's right. Let me get your file."

When she had found the bills for the delinquent

taxes, the clerk added them up. Then she asked Mrs. Wright how much she wanted to pay.

"I think five dollars," Mrs. Wright replied. She opened her billfold to the thin sheaf of one-dollar bills.

One at a time she took five out and then placed them on the counter. Then she noticed that she still had some more in the billfold. She told the clerk not to write the receipt because maybe she could spare 10. She counted out five more dollars.

There were still more dollar bills in the purse. Strange! She counted out another five. And still there were more. What was happening? Perhaps she should just take bills out until she saw only a few left. She began piling them one at a time on the counter.

The clerk was watching sharply, counting each bill as it was placed on the growing pile. It was like watching a performer taking handkerchiefs out of an empty hat, because already there were too many bills to ever go back into the billfold.

Finally Mrs. Wright saw that there were only three more dollars in the billfold. She looked up and met the clerk's puzzled eyes.

"If you can dig up 50 cents," the clerk said, "you'll have the whole bill paid. I've been counting. There are 147 dollar bills here."

"No! There can't be that many!" Mrs. Wright cried.

"Yes, there are. I counted them as you put them down."

"Well, here is another dollar."

The clerk placed 50 cents on the pile of bills and handed the other half dollar back to Mrs. Wright. "Just take this across to the treasury window and pay there," the clerk directed, handing Mrs. Wright the delinquent bills.

The cashier was surprised to see Mrs. Wright back so soon. "Why didn't you pay when you were here the first time?" she asked.

To this, all Mrs. Wright could answer was, "I don't know."

One by one the cashier counted the 147 dollar bills. The 50-cent piece finished the count. Stamping the bill "Paid in full," she handed it over with a question in her eyes.

Mrs. Wright had a question in her own eyes too. Her mind was such a swirl of impossibilities that she left the window in a trance. Moving to a little table, she began searching through her purse.

The tithe envelope still had the exact amount she had put in it. Her billfold had two dollars in the paper-money section. No. No. That billfold could never have held even a fourth of that immense pile of bills on the counter. Only God could have done this thing.

Closing her purse she bowed her head to say a sincere "Thank You, Father." Then returning to her car, she drove home rejoicing. She knew that in spite of what some people said, God was not dead. Only a living God of love could have performed this miracle just to help a poor widow woman.

10

God Prepared a Great Fish

by Ruth Robartson

K arsatoa looked down into the canoe. Did he have everything he needed for the trip? No, the lamp. It would soon be dark, and it was safer to travel at night with a light.

Karsatoa returned to the hut and called out to his companion, "Toban, bring the light when you come. The canoe is ready now."

Toban, wearing a white lap lap and carrying the lamp and his Bible, strode out of the hut and down the sandy beach to the waiting canoe. A few moments later two heads were bowed in prayer asking for guidance on the journey ahead.

Karsatoa and Toban were on their way to visit a village of new believers several miles down the coast of New Britain. They had heard persistent rumors that natives of a neighboring village a few miles away were greatly angered by the missionaries' presence and had pledged themselves to kill the two men. Karsatoa and Toban had planned the trip so that they would pass the village when everyone would be asleep.

Once the sun set, darkness was upon them with a leap, as it seems to do in tropical regions. Karsatoa lit the small lamp and placed it in the prow of the boat because of the many treacherous outcroppings of coral and other hazards in the water. The men proceeded as quickly as the darkness would permit them until they neared the hostile village. Then they turned down the lamp as low as they dared and began to slip slowly and silently past.

Just then there was a sound of disturbed water and a great dark shadow rose to the surface. Toban stopped paddling and watched in fascination at the huge stingray that lay almost motionless in the still water. He had never seen one so close before, nor so big.

Then in the stillness another sound reached their ears, a strange soft swishing of many paddles. It was too dark to see anything outside the dim circle of light cast by their small lamp.

Surely they must have been mistaken. But no, there it was again, that stealthy dip and swish. But where was it coming from? In front of them, behind on the shore side, or on the seaward side? It seemed to be coming from all four sides at once! They were surrounded!

The villagers must have waited for them. Now

that they could clearly see the forms of the two missionaries in the boat they would hurl their spears. Karsatoa and Toban reacted at once and both stabbed at the water with swift sure strokes. Perhaps they could elude their pursuers.

Then everything happened at once. The prow of a canoe shot forward into the circle of their light, and at the same time there was a boiling of turbulent water at the rear of Karsatoa's canoe. Then came a rush of wind as a great dark creature rose from the water and hurled itself into the air.

The two men flung themselves into the bottom of the canoe. Dampness from the huge stingray's body swept over them. Then there was a crash, and they were in darkness. The creature's body had struck their lamp and extinguished it.

What were they to do now? They groped around in the darkness for their hastily abandoned paddles. Before they could pick them up, they felt the canoe rise up out of the water and begin to move. Slowly at first, then with increasing speed. It seemed as if they were almost flying over the water.

"Are you paddling?" Karsatoa whispered.

"No," answered Toban. "Are you?"

"No," breathed Karsatoa, almost too afraid to speak.

Toban glanced cautiously over the side of the canoe. There, just visible below the canoe, was the black hulk of the stingray. The men had never before had such a ride. The salty mist whipped past their faces as the canoe raced across the surface of the water. When they had left their pursuers many miles behind, the great fish sank slowly beneath the rippling water, leaving the canoe becalmed.

Sitting there in the stillness, the two missionaries bowed their heads and gave praise and thanks to God for saving their lives in such a wonderful way. The same God who had prepared a great fish to rescue Jonah had also worked a miracle for them.

11

The Neighboring Railroad

by Chrystal Gee

O nly the brooder coop and scattered trees stood between our home and the railroad. From our front yard we could easily read the bold letters that said "Railroad Crossing." The wooden "X" fastened high on its pole told pedestrians and motorists that a train might pass that way. No lights blinked or flashed to indicate the arrival of a train. So when the train neared the little country crossing, the engineer blew his whistle and sometimes rang the bell that swung on top of the engine.

The train did not run every day. In fact we saw or heard it only twice a week—once going west and once going east. Usually it went to South Haven in the afternoon and returned to Kalamazoo that night or the next morning. It never came on Monday, so we knew when we tumbled out of bed that morning that we wouldn't hear a rumble, a whistle, or a chuga-chuga that day.

Soft snow had transformed our little settlement of Pine Grove into a winter wonderland weeks before. The sky was almost obliterated this December morning as large white flakes pelted toward earth and landed on trees, roofs, cars, roads, fences, posts, and fields. Even so, we were cozy and warm inside as we knelt down to pray that morning.

"And dear God, take care of us all this day," my husband ended his prayer. It was the usual closing, but we could not know how much we would be needing our heavenly Father's ever-present protection before the day was over.

At the door we kissed our red-haired daughter, Sylvia, goodbye as she left for school. How thankful we were for a 10-grade church school to send her to, and for kind neighbors who willingly let her ride with their children.

Our car had given out several months before, and our only mode of transportation was a half-ton pickup that my brother Lyle had nicknamed "Bucket of Bolts." On one side we had to roll the window down and reach outside to open the door, and on the other side the door sometimes stuck, but we were thankful for the old truck.

Today we were especially happy. We were in the chicken business, and a man had bargained for a full load. I fairly flew about my morning work, constantly looking out the window for the arrival of a truck filled with crates.

It was after lunch when my husband saw it coming. He motioned for the driver to pull in near the west-end door of our brooder coop. The top of the load just cleared the snow-covered limbs as the truck came to a stop under two large maples.

Two men opened the doors and stepped down from the cab. After talking to my husband for a minute, one of them climbed onto the back of the truck and dropped empty crates to the other man. He caught and stacked them on the ground between the truck and brooder house. My husband picked one up and took it inside.

I hurried to the coop, and we caught and crated chickens while the men loaded them onto their big truck. By mid-afternoon we had exchanged a load of noisy chickens for a handful of much-needed dollars. After a recheck on the money, the men drove away.

Back in the house we completed a third count of the money. I glanced at the clock—2:45!

"Hurry, honey," I called to my husband who was changing his clothes in the bedroom. "We'll make it to the bank if we go right now."

We raced to our good old "Bucket of Bolts" and headed down the road. In no time at all we reached the railroad tracks. Apparently a work crew had picked and chopped the packed snow and ice, then shoveled it away from the tops and sides of the rails, making the tracks look like two trenches across the road.

As our front wheels rolled over the first hump they dropped into trench number one. The back wheels started to spin on the icy downgrade. My husband tried reverse, but the truck stood still. Again the wheels spun around and around, but in the opposite direction.

"It's a good thing it isn't a train day," my husband said with a smile. "Think you can open your door and give me a push?"

"Sure." I turned to open my window so I could reach outside and open my door, but it was frozen. Glancing up, I saw the black nose of a train creeping around the bend.

"A train's coming!" I yelled. "And my window's frozen! I can't get to the door latch!" I was still struggling to open it, but it wouldn't budge. The train's whistle pierced our ears.

"Come my way," my husband said. I crowded behind him, ready to jump the second he got his door open. He worked the handle and pushed frantically with his knees, but the door refused to budge. I could see the train bearing down on us. Its whistle was wide open, its bell clanging and brakes screeching.

"Pray, Chrystal!" my husband shouted, but I already was! He pushed his foot down full force on the gas. Suddenly the pickup seemed to lift out of the trench like a helicopter. Staying just above the ground, it shot right over trench number two and settled down on the road.

Looking back I saw the truck's tailgate being cleared by mere inches as the huge iron engine, followed by two freight cars and a caboose, rumbled on its way. I looked for the dozen strong men who had rescued us, but there was no one in sight.

My husband pulled to the side of the road and stopped in front of a vacant lot. We were shaking too much to even think about getting our money to the bank. As he turned the engine off, he studied my face and asked in a husky voice, "Did you feel what I felt?"

"I did . . . if . . . if you felt as though some super being lifted the truck, shoved us forward, and set us down clear of the tracks."

"Exactly!" he exclaimed.

We bowed our heads and thanked God for answering our prayers. We knew He had taken care of us.

12

The Long Way

by Charles Rennard

Noel de Dianous struggled to shake off the guilty feeling as he headed his horse toward Julio's Bar. He wasn't such a bad fellow, he kept reassuring himself. But the unpleasant scene earlier that day still haunted his mind.

Maybe he shouldn't have become so angry after finding his wife and the people next door having Sunday school again under the mango tree in the back yard. He had a strong suspicion that they worshiped together every week in his absence. But Sunday school on *Saturday*, not Sunday! The whole idea seemed ridiculous.

Noel had married Lodi a year and a half before. He loved her dearly and wanted to be a good husband and father. But Noel's big problem was religion.

"Easy, Lady," he calmed his horse as a rabbit

hopped out into the road, twitching its nose.

I need religion about as much as that rabbit, Noel stormed to himself. *Oh, it might be all right for women and children, but I don't need it.*

He did, however, wish that he hadn't yelled so loudly at the small group that morning. Remembering the sad look Lodi had sent his way, and seeing the neighbors hurriedly leaving, he had felt like a bully. Lodi hadn't said a cross word. None of them had. And worst of all, he suspected that they were praying for him right now!

They were always trying to push religion into his life, he thought. He wanted none of it, for sure; but why not let them have their little get-together each Saturday—or Sabbath as they called it? Not that the day was of any importance. One day was just as good, or as bad, as another.

Having finally decided this, Noel began to feel more cheerful. The warm South American sun and the lush tropical forest had a soothing effect on his mind. No, he wasn't such a bad fellow after all.

In fact, Noel could have been a good provider for his wife. He had risen to a position of prestige in the oil business and made more money than most Venezuelans. But the greater part of his earnings failed to reach home because he spent so much on liquor at Julio's Bar.

Nearing the end of his 12-mile ride, Noel urged

Lady on. The sun was just beginning to sink behind the purple-hued Venezuelan hills, and he was eager to have a drink with Juan, Carlos, and Mano. That would promptly restore his confidence. Then he could go home early to cheer up Lodi and help her forget all the yelling he had done in the morning.

Noel tied his horse to the hitching post of Julio's Bar and made his way through the familiar swinging doors.

"Over here, Noel," called Carlos, and a moment later the four men were having a grand time over their drinks.

Noel enjoyed the hours they spent together at the bar. *This is truly living to the full,* he told himself.

He laughed and joked with the rest of them until some flippant remark of his unexpectedly angered Mano. Noel tried to calm his friend, but instead, further offended him. Mano cursed Noel soundly and stalked out of the bar. A rather subdued party remained, and soon the three bade one another goodbye to start their separate journeys homeward.

As Noel unhitched his horse he lingered a moment, taking in the beauty of the full, pale-white moon. It must be later than he had realized! Lodi would be worried if he didn't arrive home before 11:00. Quickly mounting Lady, he began the long ride home.

The miles passed quickly to the clippety-clop of

Lady's hooves as horse and rider covered the first few miles. But the last part was more difficult. The road divided a short distance ahead, and the fork Noel usually took was deeply wooded. The tall, dense-growing jungle trees blocked out any available moonlight, making his journey eerie.

Halfway along his trek was a small bridge, which gave the route the name Bridge Road. He was always eager to complete this particular stretch because once beyond the bridge, the road widened, and travel was easier. It was also less rocky, and the trees allowed the moonlight to illuminate the way.

A short distance before the turn down the dark and lonely Bridge Road, Noel sensed someone behind him. Before he even had time to turn and look, however, a white-clad horseman moved alongside him.

"Noel," the mysterious stranger said, "I have been sent to warn you not to travel home your usual way. Go straight; do not turn down Bridge Road."

A little frightened at first and puzzled as to how the stranger knew his name, Noel was most perturbed by the warning. "But if I go straight ahead, that road will take me several miles out of my way! Besides, my wife will be worrying about me."

"No, my friend," the white-clad rider continued, "do not turn right when the road divides."

Again Noel tried to argue, but the rider and horse

had vanished. He looked around but could see no trace of the pair.

He patted his horse to recapture his confidence. "Lady, everybody knows that no one rides around dressed in white, telling a fellow which road to take home." He knew he hadn't drunk that much. He must have been dreaming! But if the experience was real . . . No, it couldn't have been.

It still gave him a strange feeling, though, and for a moment he almost decided to take the longer route home. But he was a brave man—too brave to be intimidated by a dream.

When he reached the fork in the road, Noel hesitated only slightly before making a right turn onto Bridge Road. But he couldn't keep the stranger's warning out of his mind. And for some reason, even the trees seemed darker and more foreboding than usual.

What was that rustling in the underbrush? Just the wind surely; but odd he hadn't noticed it before now. And he had never observed the strange shapes the trees assumed in the darkness, either. Noel gave a start as his horse stumbled over a rock, then caught herself before falling.

"Steady there, Lady," he cautioned. Then, relieved to hear the reassuring sound of his own voice, he told himself, "It's all because of that fanciful warning—my imagination's gone wild. There's nothing to be afraid of."

Then his eyes opened wide, and Noel rubbed them to erase the illusion. It couldn't be, but . . . Yes—the white-clad rider and horse were right beside him again!

"Noel, you're a stubborn man. Follow me." The stranger's voice—smooth, melodious, and the most pleasant Noel had ever heard—held a tone of authority not to be ignored. He didn't reply, but meekly allowed the stranger to grasp Lady's reins, and together they rode off the road into the thick tropical forest.

At this Noel started to protest because he knew there were no other roads in the area. But to his amazement they were picking their way down a faint but definable pathway. The stranger's knowledge was incredible! But how could they possibly avoid getting hopelessly lost in the tangled maze that constantly rose before them?

The two riders continued to scramble up and down small ravines, around dark boulders, and between the dense trees and jungle growth, until they finally emerged into a large clearing. There was something very familiar about it. Why, of course! He lived just over the rise.

"Thank you very much, amigo, whoever—" But the white-clad rider and his horse were gone.

A sober and thoughtful Noel put Lady in the barn and stole quietly into the house. He didn't mention his encounter with the strange rider to his wife. He didn't want to worry her or listen to her pass it off as having something to do with religion. No, he didn't want to risk that. But Noel couldn't forget the experience.

The next day he rode out to the field in search of the mysterious path he had traveled the night before. There was no sign of a path through the dense jungle. It would have been impossible to ride through the tangled growth—even by daylight! He couldn't understand any of the eerie, inconceivable happenings of the previous night's journey.

A few days later, when he again visited Julio's Bar, Mano eyed him silently for a long time. "How did you know?" he finally asked.

"How did I know what?" answered a puzzled Noel.

"Not to go home last Saturday night."

"But I did go home Saturday night."

"Oh, no, you didn't!" Mano indignantly spat out the words. "I waited and waited under the bridge you had to pass over, and you never came."

"But, no—" Noel began, only to be interrupted.

"Noel, I know you didn't go home. Remember when we quarreled here last Saturday?"

Noel nodded.

"Well, I was so angry that I decided to ambush and kill you on your way home."

Noel's face paled. He knew his friend had a fiery temper. And he was remembering the mysterious horse and rider with the strange warning.

"But, Mano, I don't believe you," he protested. "We're good friends."

Mano hung his head. "I know, but I was too drunk to think clearly. Come with me, and I'll prove it to you."

They rode down the road and turned onto Bridge Road. When they reached the bridge they both dismounted.

"Look at this." Mano kicked a small pile of cigarette butts. "I waited here for you all Saturday night to kill you when you rode home."

Noel nodded solemnly.

"I'm glad you didn't come, though," Mano added hastily.

"I went home, all right, but by a longer way. I guess I'm lucky I did."

"What longer way? Nothing you say makes sense, Noel. You always go home on this road!"

Noel just nodded his head. How could he possibly explain what he couldn't even comprehend himself?

Little did Noel then realize that God had already begun answering the prayers of the faithful little group that met under the mango tree each week for Sabbath school. Nor could he see that the One who sent the strange rider to save his life, would guide him along still longer paths that would wind through many years of resisting and learning. Paths that would lead Noel with his wife and seven children across many countries to a new land—the United States of America—and to a life of service in proclaiming the Sabbath and all of God's last message.

But now he knows. And he's glad he followed the Lord all the long, long way.

The Clock That Struck 13

by Russell Holt

Captain Jarvis hurried through the empty town of Plymouth, past the great clock in the center of the square. Although he couldn't see its face clearly in the darkness, he was certain it must be nearly midnight. As if in answer to his thoughts, the large clock began booming out the hour. Jarvis stopped to count, partly from habit and partly because he wanted to be sure how late it really was.

As he stopped, he noticed a man standing on the corner of the square. The stranger was also obviously counting each bong of the clock. Eight, nine, 10, 11, 12, 13.

Thirteen! Captain Jarvis shook his head. He had never known the clock to make such a mistake before. Something must be wrong. The man on the corner came toward him.

"Rather unusual, I say, isn't it?" he asked in a nasal voice. He peered up at the captain. "I've never heard a clock strike 13 instead of 12."

"Nor have I," Jarvis replied. "And I've lived in this town for 30 years." He looked into the upturned face with its full beard, noticeably red even in the pale moonlight, long crooked nose, and deep-set eyes that faded into dark circles under thick eyebrows.

The stranger spoke again. "Something in the mechanism needs adjusting, I'll be bound." And with that he moved down the darkened street.

Several weeks later Captain Jarvis awoke much earlier than he normally did. For several minutes he lay in bed staring at the dark ceiling. Then because he couldn't sleep, he got up and dressed. Going down the stairs, he opened the front door of his house, and to his surprise there stood Oliver, his groom, with his horse all saddled and ready for him to mount.

Oliver wore a puzzled look. "I couldn't sleep, sir," he answered his master's unspoken question. "I had a strong feeling you would be wanting your horse. I tried to ignore it, knowing that you never go out so early, sir, but the feeling just got stronger and stronger. So finally I got up and prepared the horse for you."

The captain didn't know what to make of this, but he climbed onto the horse and rode away from the house. He put the bridle down and decided to let the horse go wherever he chose. Indeed, the horse seemed to be as sure of his destination as his owner was uncertain. Straight to the riverside he went.

When they came to the spot where the ferryboat took passengers across, the captain was in for another surprise. Although the sun wasn't up yet, the ferryman was there, waiting to take him across.

"Why are you here so early, my man?" inquired Captain Jarvis in amazement.

"I don't know, sir," he replied, "except that I couldn't sleep this morning. The longer I tried to rest in my bed, the more I felt I should get up and bring the boat across, that someone would need to pass over the river. I had just gotten the boat here when you arrived, sir." He jumped forward to help the captain on board.

A few minutes later a wondering captain stood with his horse on the far side of the river, while an equally puzzled ferryman went back to his little cabin beside the water.

Captain Jarvis swung into the saddle, allowing the horse once again to go where he pleased. Horse and rider started off at a brisk trot as the sun rose and climbed into the morning sky. While his horse turned down one road and then another, the captain wondered what the outcome of these strange events might be.

Why was Oliver impressed to ready my horse so

early? he asked himself. *And why was the ferryman waiting for me before the sun was up?*

Captain Jarvis lost sight of his surroundings while he turned these things over in his mind. But after a bit he shook his head clear and noticed that they were entering a country town.

"Hello!" he called, stopping a passerby in the dusty street. "Is anything unusual happening in town today?"

The man paused to recollect. "Not particularly. The court is meeting to try a man for murder, over there." And he pointed out a stone building.

Captain Jarvis rode over and dismounted. Quietly he slipped through the back door of the courtroom. Evidently the trial was almost over. In front of the room the judge was addressing the prisoner.

"Have you anything to say for yourself before the sentencing—anything at all?"

As the accused man stood to face the judge, Captain Jarvis gave a little gasp. There was no mistaking the full red beard, the deep-set eyes, and long crooked nose, nor the nasal voice when he spoke.

"I have nothing to say, sir, except that I am an innocent man. There is only one person in all the world who could prove my innocence, but I do not know his name, or where he is. Some weeks ago we stood together in the town of Plymouth at midnight, and we both heard the town clock strike 13 instead of 12. We remarked about it to each other. If he were here, he could speak for me, but my case is hopeless. Only God could answer my prayer and bring him here."

"I am here! I am here!" shouted the captain from the back of the room. "I am the man who stood at midnight beside the Plymouth clock and heard it strike 13 instead of 12. What the prisoner says is absolutely true. I identify him as the man. On the night of the murder, at the very time it was committed, that man was with me at Plymouth. We mentioned to each other how remarkable it was that the clock should strike 13 at midnight!"

The judge pronounced the condemned man innocent and set him free. Then Captain Jarvis understood who had awakened him and the groom and the ferryman. He knew who had guided his horse. He knew who had caused the clock to strike 13.

14

Miracle of the Missing Money

by Goldie Down

A cool breeze ruffled the palm fronds and carried the salty smell of the sea to Biribo's nostrils as he shuffled his bare feet in the warm sand. For hours he had been standing on the shore straining his eyes seaward.

Out beyond the lagoon, beyond the reef that surrounded it like a protecting wall, beyond the frothy white spray ceaselessly fountaining skyward, the Pacific Ocean lay blue and deep. Biribo knew that somewhere out there his father was paddling homeward. It had been three days since he had gone off in his little canoe to the mission headquarters to collect his monthly pay.

For a few minutes Biribo's attention wandered to the far end of the island where some of the men and boys were preparing to go out to the reef after octopus. When he looked back at the blue horizon he saw a tiny black speck. It must be Father coming!

Biribo's heart thumped with excitement as he watched the speck grow bigger and bigger and gradually resolve itself into the shape of a canoe. Yes, it was his father.

"He's coming. He's coming." Biribo flew up the sandy path to the village.

"Father's coming!" he yelled as he scrambled up the notched trunk that served as steps to the palm-thatched platform that was his home.

Biribo's mother was sitting cross-legged on the floor plaiting leaf mats. She gave an excited cry and, gathering the baby under her arm, she raced back with Biribo to the shore.

The canoe could now be seen plainly. They stood waving and calling, although they knew that their voices wouldn't be heard above the roar of the waves.

Father didn't wave back. He was too busy holding his paddle and watching the sea while he waited for just the right swell to carry his frail craft over the treacherous reef. If the wave wasn't high enough, both he and the canoe would be swamped.

The canoe bounced and bucked as if it were alive as Father held it in check until the right wave rolled in. Mother held her breath, and Biribo murmured a quick prayer for Father's safety as they watched the battle between man and ocean.

A large wave came rolling behind Father, and he struggled to keep the stern of the canoe toward it. The wave rose like a blue-green wall, and he was lost to sight as the water lifted the little craft and propelled it forward. When the white spray subsided Biribo could see the canoe skimming rapidly across the calm waters of the lagoon.

As Father neared the shore, Biribo waded into the water to help him beach the canoe. Mother and baby ran forward to greet him, and Father smiled at them and took the baby in his arms. But almost immediately Biribo sensed that something was wrong. Father's smile was only on his lips. His eyes looked worried and sad.

Mother noticed it too. "Did you have any trouble?" she asked as she picked up the paddle. They all turned to walk up the tree-lined path.

Father didn't answer at once. He stared straight ahead as if he were looking at something miles away. Finally he said quietly, "I've lost the pay packet."

Mother drew in a quick breath but said nothing. They weren't likely to starve because there were plenty of fish in the sea and coconuts on the trees, but they needed money for salt and soap and cooking oil and matches.

"How did you lose it, Father?" Biribo shooed a stray chicken from the front of their hut, and they all clambered up the palm trunk and squatted on the rough floor.

"I don't know." Father's voice was husky. "I tucked the envelope into my belt when I got into the canoe. It must have fallen out while I was paddling. I've searched everywhere in the canoe, and it isn't there." He looked down at his simple skirt-like garment. "Perhaps if I had had a shirt and trousers with many pockets, it would have been safe."

Silence fell in the little home. Even the baby seemed to know that something was wrong.

"Maybe it will float ashore," suggested Biribo hopefully. "Sometimes we find things thrown up on the beach. We can go every day and look for it."

"One tiny brown envelope in that vast ocean?" Father's tone showed how foolish Biribo's suggestion was. "Besides, there were some silver coins as well as the paper money. Their weight would have carried the packet clear down to the bottom of the sea."

Biribo tried again. "We can pray."

Father looked at Mother, and she said, "Yes, we can pray. The Bible says that God made an iron ax head swim, so He can make silver money float if He wants to."

A glimmer of hope shone in Father's eyes. "Of course He can. God knows where our money is, and He knows how much we need it. Let's pray right now."

Baby plumped down on her fat little knees with the others. Father prayed first, and then Mother and Biribo. They all asked God to please send the money to them if it was His will. Even on their remote island it would be hard to get along without money for an entire month.

As soon as it was daylight the next morning Biribo rushed down to the beach to search for the missing money. Perhaps it had been washed ashore during the night.

Carefully he went up and down the beach, turning over every stone and large shell, sifting the sand through his bare brown toes. There was no sign of the money.

Undaunted, the little family prayed again. Morning, noon, and at evening they prayed that God would send the money to them, and with every prayer their faith became stronger. They *knew* that God would send the money somehow.

On the second morning Biribo searched even more carefully, crisscrossing the sand with the tracks of his bare feet. Still there was no sign of the money.

That afternoon Biribo took his baby sister with him. She sat on the sand and played with a handful of shells while he hunted carefully along the water's edge and into every crack and crevice of the rocks near the shore. Still no money.

Biribo sighed as he sat down on the sand near his sister. He hoped that God would send the money soon because Mother's oil bottle was empty and only 10 matches remained in the box. He had counted them that morning while she was coaxing the cooking fire into flame. Father was so busy with his mission work that he had no time to try to earn any money by fishing.

For a little while Biribo amused the baby by covering her short legs with mounds of sand and letting her wriggle her toes and kick until she was free again. Then she began to cover his legs while he leaned back on his elbows and drowsily watched the gentle wavelets lapping the shore of the lagoon.

Farther out near the reef, sea birds dipped and soared. There must be a shoal of fish nearby. Yes, he could see small dark patches on the surface of the blue lagoon. But were they fish? Biribo's forehead creased as he strained to see.

Suddenly he leaped up and sent sand spraying under his running feet. His baby sister cried out with surprise at his abrupt movements and turned to watch him. Straight into the water Biribo splashed, grabbing and clutching at the bits of paper that were floating toward him. Tears mingled with the salt spray on his cheeks, and yet he laughed—laughed and shouted as he gathered up the money that God had sent.

Stopping only long enough to hoist his little sister onto his hip, Biribo ran home. "It's come," he cried as he pushed the baby up the steps. "Mother, Father, the money has come! God has sent it."

There was no sign of the brown envelope, but

when Father counted the paper money that had floated ashore he found that only one note was missing—and the silver coins.

Oh, what prayers of praise and thanksgiving bubbled from their grateful hearts. Mother and Father went back to the beach with Biribo, and he showed them just where he had been sitting on the sand and how he had seen the money floating ashore and had dashed into the sea to collect it.

"It was coming in right there." His voice trembled with excitement as he pointed to a spot a few feet from the shore. Then his black eyes widened, and his pointing finger stiffened with amazement. There in the very same spot, a plank of driftwood was bobbing gently toward them. And on top of the driftwood was a piece of paper money, and on top of the note—acting like a paperweight—was a little pile of silver coins!

As the driftwood slid onto the sand Father stepped forward and reverently counted the money that God had sent. It made up the exact amount of his lost pay. Not one cent was missing.

The father in this story is Pastor Lati from Tanna, who was stationed on the island of Mavia as district director of Santo in 1962 when this miracle occurred.

15

Dr. Parrot's Miracle

by Enola M. Fargusson

Oliver dished up two bowls of oatmeal and called his father to breakfast. He spooned on thick cream skimmed from the milk cans in the pantry and began to eat hungrily. Pa nibbled a few bites and then put down his spoon.

"Ma's worse," he said.

"Do you want me to fetch Miss Hubbard?" Oliver asked.

"No, I think you'd better ride into Windsor and ask Dr. Parrot to come over."

"Pa," Ma called weakly from the bedroom. "It's too far for Oliver to go alone."

Pa got up and went over to the bedroom door. "The boy's 16," he said. "Besides, Dr. Parrot came to our baptisms. She said to call on her if we ever needed help."

Oliver hurried to the barn before Ma could change Pa's mind. At least going for the doctor would give him something to do. He'd felt so helpless ever since Ma had become sick. Riding one horse and leading another one for the doctor, he set out for Windsor.

"If you ask me," he said to himself, "it's all the fault of those preachers. First they come here and addle folks' brains with fables from the Bible and pictures of weird beasts. Then they dunk them in the icy waters of the creek. No wonder Ma got sick. How can people fall for that stuff?"

Oliver had been disappointed when his parents had become believers. For the most part, he was proud of his folks. They'd built a prosperous farm in the Piner District north of San Francisco. They worked hard, and they were intelligent, level-headed people who could always poke holes in faulty arguments. But when two men, John Loughborough and Daniel Bourdeau, had begun a series of Adventist Bible lectures at the schoolhouse, Oliver's parents had accepted everything they taught.

As his parents' religious interests deepened, a rift grew between them and their son. Oliver was still loving toward them and helpful around the farm, but he laughed at their Bible studies and refused to join them for family worship.

Oliver had been even more surprised at the conversion of the well-educated, well-traveled Dr.

Parrot. She had left her native France to attend medical school in Geneva, Switzerland. Then she'd sailed halfway around the world to northern California.

Elder Loughborough and Elder Bourdeau had held the first Adventist evangelistic series in California at nearby Petaluma in 1868. Then they had moved to Windsor, where Dr. Parrot was baptized. Afterward they had traveled to Piner, and from there had gone to Santa Rosa.

"One thing you'll have to say for these Christians," Oliver muttered to himself between bites of a sandwich in Dr. Parrot's kitchen. "They do help each other."

Dr. Parrot packed quickly, locked her house, and they set out for Piner. Oliver was entranced by the sprightly, middle-aged French doctor. He asked her questions about Europe, and she told him stories of her travels as they rode.

They were almost home when she said, "Don't worry about your mother. God loves her and will take care of her."

"Don't talk to me about God," Oliver snapped. "If He loved her, He wouldn't let her suffer."

"Even Christians aren't spared the ravages of sin," Dr. Parrot began.

"Sin!" Oliver answered angrily. "My mother never intentionally did a wrong thing in her life. She's always been kind and good to everyone."

"There's a purpose to everything," Dr. Parrot said. "Just put your trust in Him."

"In whom?" Oliver demanded. "Can you see Him? Can you touch Him? Can you talk to Him?"

"Yes, I can talk to Him," Dr. Parrot said. "I can pray."

"You talk to empty air," Oliver sneered. "Don't speak to me about God." They were in sight of the house now, so Oliver urged his horse into a trot, ending the conversation.

Under Dr. Parrot's care, Ma began to get better. Finally she was well enough to be out of bed most of the time and to take over some of the lighter household chores.

When the time came for Dr. Parrot to leave, several friends gathered at Oliver's home to see her off. While they knelt to ask the Lord's blessing on her journey, Oliver went to the barn to saddle the two horses. He had mixed feelings as he prepared Pa's gentlest horse for Dr. Parrot to ride. He would miss her laughter and the stories she told. But with her gone, there'd be one less person on his back about religion.

Dr. Parrot was standing on the front porch when he brought the horses around. He tied her bags to his saddle and helped her to mount up.

Suddenly the usually gentle horse began to buck and rear. Dr. Parrot pitched off sideways. The horse fell on her, and the saddle horn struck her full in the chest.

Pa and Oliver helped the horse to its feet. Oliver tied the now-docile beast to a tree while Pa knelt over Dr. Parrot and felt her pulse. Oliver saw Pa shake his head.

"Dead?" the boy cried. "She can't be!"

"Let's carry her into the house," one of the men said. "I don't think anyone could survive an injury like this."

Oliver helped the men lift Dr. Parrot off the ground. Gently they carried her in and laid her on the bed in the room she'd vacated just minutes before.

Oliver had never before seen death come so quickly. He'd known old people who'd died, children who hadn't survived birth, and people who had lingered with illness, slowly wasting away. But to be talking and laughing one minute, and gone the next—

"Wait," he cried. "Her eyes are opening."

Dr. Parrot moaned and looked around at the circle of worried faces.

"Get a doctor!" one of the men shouted.

"No," she whispered. "No doctor can help me. Get Elder Loughborough and Elder Bourdeau."

Oliver had heard about last rites, and a tear trickled down his cheek.

"If they pray for me," Dr. Parrot continued, "the Lord will heal me."

"Will you go, son?" Pa asked, putting his arm across Oliver's shoulders.

"It won't do any good, but I'll go," Oliver agreed desolately.

The boy mounted his horse and hurried to Santa Rosa, where the two men were holding evangelistic meetings. He got to the large tent just as people were filing in for the evening meeting.

Tersely, Oliver explained the accident and relayed Dr. Parrot's request for the ministers to come pray for her.

"I doubt she'll be alive when you get there," Oliver blurted. "She's really hurt badly."

Elder Loughborough looked through a tent flap at the large crowd and turned to Elder Bourdeau. "What do you think, Daniel?" he asked. "There's a big crowd out there tonight."

"I don't see how we can disappoint them by calling off the meeting," Elder Bourdeau answered thoughtfully.

"I agree," Elder Loughborough said. "It's a hard decision to make, but I'm afraid we'll have to wait until after the meeting to go see Dr. Parrot."

"Some people stay afterward to discuss the things we've brought up during the meeting, so it'll probably be early morning before we can get there," Elder Bourdeau added.

Oliver nodded and left. As he hurried back to Piner, his mind churned with turmoil. Was this all there was to life? A brief span here on earth, then oblivion? Was anyone really in charge of events? Viewing the chaos in the world, it was hard to believe. But then, what was the purpose of life if everything ended so meaninglessly?

As he approached the house, Oliver was relieved to see a light shining in Dr. Parrot's bedroom. Pa and two other men were standing near the bed. Dr. Parrot's breathing was harsh and raspy.

"Whenever she tries to move, she faints," Pa told him. "Are the ministers coming?"

"They'll be here toward morning," he answered wearily as he took off his jacket.

It was a long night. It seemed as though Dr. Parrot's every breath would be her last. But finally dawn came, and with it the sound of an approaching wagon.

Soon Elder and Mrs. Loughborough and Elder Bourdeau joined the men at Dr. Parrot's bedside. Weakly she opened her eyes and smiled.

"Perhaps the Lord will at least relieve her of some pain so that we can take her to Santa Rosa for medical care," Mrs. Loughborough said.

While she anointed Dr. Parrot, the others knelt by the bedside. The ministers commended her to the Great Physician.

Oliver had withdrawn to a corner to watch the ritual. Sorrowfully he kept his eyes on his friend's face. He saw the pain leave Dr. Parrot's face, and be replaced by peace and joy. For a moment Oliver thought she was dead. Then she began to pray along with the ministers. Suddenly she clapped her hands and sat up in bed.

"I'm healed," she said. "Praise God!" Then she looked around the room and smiled. "If you gentleman will remove yourselves, I'd like to get dressed."

The first thing she did when she came out of the bedroom was to assure Oliver's mother that she was all right. The next thing was to help the neighbor women prepare breakfast.

Afterward they put a chair in the back of the wagon so she could return to Santa Rosa with the ministers.

"I want to tell the folks at the meetings how God healed me," she said.

"Let me tell them," Oliver said. "I've been an unbeliever, but today I saw the power of God. He does hear prayers, and He does answer. I want to tell everyone that the age of miracles isn't past."

Dr. Parrot leaned over and hugged Oliver.

"We've had two miracles today," she said. "God healed me, and He made a believer out of you."

16

Extra Mileage

by Sharon R. Todd

Sixteen-year-old Joan could hardly sit still long enough for her mother to finish eating.

"Hold on, Joan," her mother remarked. "The car isn't going anywhere without us. I'm not that eager to go back outside."

The roadside diner felt nice and cool after the hot countryside they had been driving through all day. But Joan had forgotten all about the relentless sunshine the minute Mom had asked her whether she'd like to drive the car. She had driven the family wagon only a few times since getting her driver's permit, and never very far. To drive it now, pulling the camper and crossing Nevada, seemed so very grown up.

"I'd like to reach your grandmother's before her birthday, but driving all day with the air conditioner on has given me a headache. I think I need to rest awhile." Mother sipped her drink, then placed the cool glass against her forehead. "We have an open stretch ahead of us, and it's late enough so that the traffic shouldn't be too heavy. Do you really think you can handle the car with the camper on back?"

"Sure I can," Joan said. "I'd drive it with an elephant chained on the back!"

Mother laughed at her daughter's enthusiasm. "Are you sure you brought your license?"

After flashing the shiny new license for her mother to see, Joan slipped it back into her purse and reached across the table for the keys. She was already in the station wagon with her seat belt fastened and the key in the ignition by the time her mother had paid the cashier and joined her.

"Remember to go slow and easy so that you don't take any chances on jackknifing the camper."

Joan nodded. After her mother offered a short prayer for their protection, Joan eased out of the parking lot and onto the road leading back to the interstate.

Hardly daring to take her eyes off the road, Joan glanced occasionally into the rearview and side mirrors to check on the camper. With a contented smile she settled back and enjoyed the sunset that played out the last of its glorious colors before her eyes.

"Isn't that beautiful, Mom?"

But her mother lay sleeping soundly on the back seat. Feeling terribly grown up and a bit lonely, Joan flipped the radio on low. With it set at her mother's favorite "traveling" station, Joan hummed with the quiet music that filled the car.

Several miles down the road Joan noticed that the gas gauge registered slightly below the quarter mark. Knowing her mother's policy of filling up way before it hit empty, Joan began to look for a gas station. So far the only one she had passed was a small unlit store with a large "out of gas" sign.

Joan began to bite her lower lip, and worry lines creased her brow. The darkness had settled all around them, the gas gauge sank closer to the empty mark, and her mother was still sleeping soundly.

Joan flipped the right-turn signal and carefully edged the car off the highway. Then, pulling out the hazard button, she turned to touch her mother's shoulder. "Mom, Mom."

Sitting up groggily, Mother glanced out the window. "Is something wrong?"

"We're almost out of gas. The only station I've passed so far was closed."

Mother peered at the gas gauge. "How much is left?"

"Less than a quarter tank."

"Where are we?"

Joan showed her mother their position on the road map.

"Well, you'll just have to keep driving. Surely

there's a station open somewhere."

Joan signaled for a left turn and got back on the interstate. As the miles passed with no sign of another station, Joan found herself thinking about Philip's meeting the Ethiopian in the desert. "Do you think God wants us to do something special for Him, like Philip did?" she asked.

"I don't know, Joan. If He does, then He'll protect us and show us His will." With a worried glance at the unbroken darkness, Mother added thoughtfully, "I'd just as soon not be stuck out here, though." She flashed a quick smile at Joan and patted her daughter on the shoulder. "The Lord has taken good care of us so far, and I'm sure he won't stop now."

Joan smiled back at her mother. It was true that ever since her father's heart attack three months before, God had helped them get through it all. First, the funeral; then, the decision to join Joan's grandparents out West. Even finding a buyer for the house so quickly. And their long trip had been trouble free.

"Thank You, Jesus, for looking after us," Joan prayed. No matter what happened she knew that God would be with them.

Just as the needle reached the right side of the "E," lights up ahead caught Joan's eye. "Look, Mom!"

Pulling in next to the pumps, Joan let out a dismayed cry. A large "closed" sign was posted in one of the windows.

"But the lights, Mom?"

"Probably to discourage someone from breaking in."

As Joan started to pull out, Mother touched her shoulder. "Would you like me to drive?"

Joan just shrugged.

"You're doing fine. Go ahead."

As Joan stepped on the accelerator, the red needle edged farther across the "E." Finally the needle dropped below the "E" on the left side and remained fixed in that position. Joan caught her mother's eyes in the rearview mirror.

"Stop a moment please, Joan."

Pulling over to the side, mother and daughter joined hands. "Dear Lord," Mother prayed, "we are all alone in a big desert. You are our one unfailing source of help. If it be Your will, please help us to make it safely to our destination. Nevertheless, Your will, not ours, be done. In Jesus' name. Amen."

Mother held Joan's hands a moment longer. "No matter what, Joan, remember that God loves us and He'll help us, OK?"

Joan nodded and turned back to the front. Placing one hand on the wheel, Joan turned the key. The motor hummed smoothly.

Back on the road again, Joan gasped, "Mother, look!"

Mother leaned over and stared at the gas gauge.

The needle had moved from point "E" to the

other side of the word "Full."

"Is—is something wrong with the gauge?" Joan asked softly.

Mother rested her head against the back of the seat. "I don't know, Joan. But I do know that the Lord is with us."

On and on they drove, passing two more stations with "closed" signs in front of them. The needle didn't budge from its far-right position, nor did the car give a sign of running low on gas.

Just as a faint tinge of sunlight glowed on the mountaintops far, far ahead, Joan called out, "Look, Mom. Am I dreaming? That station is all lit up, and I think I see cars being waited on."

It was no dream. At last they had reached an open gas station. And as they parked next to the gas pumps, the needle slowly sank back to the left and came to rest below the "E."

"Mom, we still have the camper, don't we?" Joan glanced into the rearview mirror. Sure enough, the camper was there.

"Why?" A puzzled look crossed her mother's face.

"The car's been running so smoothly since we stopped to pray that it felt like there wasn't any weight on it."

Mother's eyes welled with tears, and a smile chased all the worry lines far away. "I had the same feeling. God is so good!"

Joan sat in thoughtful silence.

As the gas attendant came to the window for his money, he shoved his cap back and rubbed his forehead. "That gas tank was so empty I didn't think I'd ever fill it up. What have you folks been running on?"

Joan and Mother exchanged looks. "Prayers," Joan answered with a big grin. "Prayers and angel power."

17

Canoe Trip
With an Angel

by Dawn Hoerner

Little Miami River was usually a great place to canoe, but there had been so much rain the past few weeks that the Frisby family was told that the river was unsafe. Finally the Sunday afternoon came when the owner of the boat rental place said it was safe for canoeing.

Father, Mother, Lisa, and Jerry had just recently come to know the Lord. As Lisa strapped on her life jacket, she said, "Dad, shouldn't we ask for God's protection before we go?"

The family bowed their heads and prayed as they stood by the wide expanse of shiny smooth water. Since the family had been canoeing only once before, it took a little while to get the craft to go where they wanted it to. Mother sat in the front and Dad guided from the rear while Lisa and Jerry sat quietly in the middle.

As they traveled down river, they noticed that there were many sections of white water rapids across rugged rocks.

"We're going really fast, aren't we, Dad?" asked Jerry.

"Yes, the current is pretty strong. I think the river must still be higher than normal."

"Didn't there used to be a danger sign on that far bank?" asked Mother. "The high waters must have swept it away."

"I don't like all these rapids," added Lisa. "They scare me!"

"God's protecting us so let's enjoy the beautiful nature," encouraged her father.

Just then the river opened into a wide, peaceful-looking area. The canoe still didn't behave very well, but it was much easier to maneuver in the smooth waters.

Suddenly they saw a large fallen tree looming up ahead in the middle of the deep water, its limbs pointing in the same direction as the current.

"Let's be careful as we go around it," called Mother. "I can see more white water beyond the tree."

"That certainly is a big tree," observed Father as they came closer. "Must be about 30 feet long."

Just then the current grabbed the boat and aimed them straight toward the twisted tree roots sticking out of the water.

Lisa, seeing their danger, gripped the boat sides and prayed silently for protection.

Splash! In an instant the canoe flipped over, throwing Mother off to one side and Father and the two children off to the other.

Father's first thoughts were for the children, who had disappeared under the dark water. What if they were under the boat? How could he get it turned over? But somehow the canoe was suddenly upright, even though it was half full of water. Father looked inside, but neither Lisa nor Jerry was visible.

As he clung to the canoe and wondered what to do next, he saw Lisa's blond head pop to the surface right in front of him. With two fingertips he grabbed the very edge of her life jacket. It was impossible in the swift current to get a better hold.

Lisa smiled weakly. "I'm OK, Dad."

If Father had let go of the boat, he might have been able to get a better grip on Lisa, but he just couldn't make his hand release the boat. *How strange*, he thought. He continued to grasp the boat and barely hang on to Lisa as they were swept along the side of the tree.

He looked in the boat again, and there, waist deep in water, sat Jerry!

"Jerry, you're safe! How did you get in there?" Father felt almost weak with relief.

"I don't know, Dad. I guess my angel put me here."

The branches of the tree were right in front of them now, and Lisa grabbed for a big one. She clung to it so that her father could use both hands to hold on to the canoe. He wondered how they were still by the tree when the current was so swift. Also, he realized that if he had released the canoe, Jerry would have been carried to the cruel white water. The three of them pulled themselves onto the trunk of the tree.

But where was Mother? After she had been thrown out, Mother found herself being pulled down and under the tree by the undercurrent. At that moment she knew she would die. "Lord, into Your hands I give my life," she prayed one more time.

The next thing she knew, she was sitting on the fallen tree! How had she possibly gotten there? Her left leg hurt so terribly that she could barely move it. She knew she couldn't have climbed the tree herself. She was convinced that her guardian angel had been there to save her life. A trembling and thankful woman looked around for her family and spotted them at the far end of the tree.

After a few minutes two men came along in a canoe. They helped Father empty the water from his canoe and then went to get a rescue team.

As the family sat waiting on the tree in the middle of the river, each one said a prayer of thanks for God's great protection. Father realized that he had lost his wallet, so in his prayer he added, "Lord, if it is Your will, let someone find the wallet—someone who needs the money."

Several days later, when everyone was rested and Mother's broken leg was in a cast, a phone call came.

"I found your wallet along the bank of the river," said a man's voice.

"Thank you. You must have a special need for money right now," answered Father.

"How did you know?" asked the man in surprise. "I've been praying about it for the last few days."

Father explained and then said, "Take half the money in the wallet as a reward. The other half I'm going to give as a special thank offering at church!"

18

Day of Miracles

by Dave Fairchild

Picture yourself in Africa. Not in the lush rain forests of the Congo, but on the dusty plains of Southern Africa during the dry season. The red soil puffs up from beneath your tramping feet and settles down in swirling clouds.

A year ago a new mission station was built here, along with the usual little school building covered with a corrugated tin roof. Response was slow at first, but soon enough students attended to make a mission vegetable garden necessary.

Cassava and yams spread their leaves over the ground. Corn and beans stretched out in long rows. Surrounding the mission borders, the gardens of the local people stood tall and healthy—acre upon acre of cool green shade.

Every day the villagers called their greetings to

the Christian students who worked the mission garden or attended classes. Noticing the stream of people passing around noon each day, the mission director questioned one of his students.

"Megijinyelwa, where do all these people go every day? Is there another garden to the west that needs hoeing?"

The young man smiled. "No, there is no garden. They visit the shrine of an ancient god, the god of wind and rain. He is believed to be the most powerful god within many days' walk from here, and he must be prayed to every day."

During the weeks that followed, Pastor Larsen tried to convince the villagers that the god they visited was only a superstition.

"The real God of wind and rain is the God of our mission, the one we tell our students about. Please come and spend some time here instead of at your shrine with a god who can't hear or see you."

But few listened, and most just shook their heads at the "crazy" missionary. Everyone knew that the god of the shrine was much more powerful than any stranger's god could ever be. So the stream of people continued on into the long hot months of the dry season.

The days went by, and the sun continued to burn from a brilliant blue sky. No rain fell, and the sky remained cloudless week after dusty week. Villagers and students alike began to worry as the dark-green of the gardens began to fade. The leaves turned brown and withered.

The crowd passing by at noon increased, each villager bearing some offering for the god at the shrine. At the mission the students and teachers joined in prayer, asking God for rain before it was too late. Neither group experienced any success.

The villagers' friendly greetings continued, but now they were tinged with frustration and sarcasm. "If your god is the one true God, why is there no rain for your beans and corn?" Some of the newer students began to weaken, and they whispered the villagers' questions among themselves.

Three more days of parching heat went by. Then one noon Pastor Larsen stepped out onto his porch and gazed out over the mission garden, now yellowish-brown instead of green. An old man's call from the nearby road attracted his attention.

"Good morning, Sir Director. Has your god made any rain lately?" Before Pastor Larsen could reply, the voice continued. "I see your gardens are as dry as ours. You tell us that your god is stronger than the god of my village. All right, then. *I challenge him!*"

His last words had risen to a shout easily heard throughout the mission compound. The old man shook his fist at the missionary. "We go to offer a cow and two chickens to our god so he will bring us rain. Pray to your god as you will and let us see which god will work the strongest magic!"

The grizzled warrior faded back into the crowd of villagers making their way toward the distant shrine.

Pastor Larsen quietly bowed his head for a minute, and then spoke to one of the students nearby. "Abram, call the students and teachers together for a prayer meeting in the chapel."

While they were praying, the wind began to blow. Students and missionaries dashed into the courtyard to stare at the darkening sky. In the west the sun had disappeared behind a mass of towering clouds. The stiffening wind caught those clouds, driving them eastward toward the mission and the neighboring village.

The villagers were returning from the shrine in haste, assured that their sacrifice had finally awakened the god of rain. The mission students were equally sure that their own prayer meeting had done the job. And so both groups held their breath and awaited the onrushing clouds. Whose god would work the magic?

The clouds skidded along, dark and heavy with rain. And just as they crossed the mission borders the rain fell, drenching the garden. The students cheered and held their faces up to the rain, letting it wash off the ever-present dust.

Just as suddenly the rain stopped, for the clouds had moved off the mission territory. The villagers gazed in amazement. One side of the road was dry, and the other side was wet and muddy.

With a sudden gust the wind changed, blowing westward this time. The rain clouds came to a halt, and then blew back across the mission. More rain fell, but only on the mission, leaving the village as dry as ever. After reaching the western border of the compound the clouds once again held their rain in check.

But the God of the mission wasn't finished yet. Twice more the clouds made their circuit of the mission, drenching every inch with precious water. And then the clouds melted away into a once more brilliant-blue sky.

Need you be told that the village god was forgotten and that the God of the mission was accepted wholeheartedly by the villagers? The day of miracles is indeed not a thing of the past!

19

Miracle From the Sky

by Biz Fairchild

We've run out of food," the director's wife told the mission people one hot, dry afternoon. "We must remember God's promises and ask him to 'give us this day our daily bread.'" The small group knelt, and each one prayed earnestly to God, asking for the help they so desperately needed.

The mission was located in central Angola, Africa. Fifty-two people lived in this mission. Their director was away visiting the out schools that day, and his wife was in charge while he was gone. Drought had swept the land, the crops had died, water holes had dried up, and no *mealie meal* (white cornmeal, which is a staple of the African diet) could be found in anyone's cupboards.

A short time after the group had gathered for prayer, the director's wife looked in surprise at her

8-year-old daughter who had just come into the house. The little girl was munching on handfuls of small, white morsels.

"What are you eating?" the mother asked.

"Mamma, the ground outside is covered with it! Two European men came up to me and said, 'God has answered your prayers and has sent you food, just as in the days of Moses. It is manna. Take it and eat it.' So I'm eating it, and it tastes so good!"

Her mother could hardly believe it. Calling the other women, she hurried outside. Sure enough, small, irregularly shaped white lumps were scattered on the grass. The famished people gathered bowls of it, joyfully harvesting the miraculous food.

"Mamma, it tastes like honey, doesn't it?"

The director's wife smiled in answer. For the first time in days, everyone's hunger was satisfied. But even more important than that, God had worked a miracle just for their little mission village in the African forest.

The mission director's wife immediately sent for her husband. "Hurry home, Carlos!" she said. "A miracle has happened!"

He sped back to the mission and was amazed to see a kind of food that fit the biblical description of manna. The only difference was that this manna didn't spoil at the end of each day.

The heaven-sent food fell for only three days, and

only on the 40 acres of cleared land belonging to the mission. The families gathered it in big pots and had all they needed to eat for a long time, enough to last them until the drought passed and crops could be harvested again.

"I'm afraid the South African Division in Cape Province isn't going to believe this!" the mission director exclaimed to his wife one day after the miracle had occurred.

"Why don't you send them some of the manna?" his wife suggested.

And so a bowl of manna accompanied the mission director's report. Word of the "food from heaven" quickly spread. The story has been told and retold for years as convincing proof that God is just as much with His people around the world today as He was back in Bible times.

20

The Case of the Missing Footprints

by Jeris E. Bragan

It was late Tuesday afternoon, December 11, 1951. Snow was falling heavily over the Hall farm, located three miles north of Lisbon Falls, Maine. More than six inches had accumulated by the time darkness closed in at 4:00 p.m.

Charley Hall, a large, burly farmer, drove recklessly through the storm toward home. Already legally blind, he drove the fishtailing vehicle over Bowdoinham Road more from memory than skill.

He felt trapped. He had been laid off from the Bona Fide Linoleum Mill three months before, and the meager funds and food supplies he needed for his wife and five children during the winter were already running out. He'd gone into town to beg for his old job.

"I'm sorry, Charley. But we just can't put you back

on the line, not with your poor eyesight," his former boss had said an hour earlier.

Edie was peering through the living room window, watching as her father approached the house. She could tell things hadn't gone well in town from the way he slammed the car door and stomped toward the house. She dropped the curtain over the window and fled to her unheated room in the attic. She turned on her gooseneck lamp for warmth and crawled with it under the thick covers.

"Dear God, why didn't you answer my prayer for Daddy?" she prayed bitterly.

Later that evening the sound of popcorn popping in the iron pot filled the kitchen as Charley tuned the dial on an old radio to listen to his favorite network programs: *Amos and Andy*, *The Jack Benny Show*, and *Our Miss Brooks*.

Edie sat in a chair at the table, cutting paper clothes out of her book to put on her cardboard dolls. She glanced at the Christmas tree standing near the front window in the living room. She and her 13-year-old brother, Melvin, had selected the tree, cut it down, and carried it home.

Most of the decorations were handmade—except for one piece. On top of the tree stood a ceramic angel with arms outstretched toward heaven.

"Do you believe angels exist?" Edie asked Melvin in a whisper.

He shrugged. "I dunno. But they talk about 'em in church, so maybe they do."

"Charley, there's somebody at the front door," Mother called just when the clock chimed 8:00.

"Well, go see who it is and get rid of them," her husband muttered. "I don't want to talk with anybody."

A tall, bearded man stood in the enclosed entryway. Edie could see that he was neatly dressed, wearing gray flannel pants, a red-and-black checked flannel shirt, and a heavy woolen navy jacket with the large collar turned up to protect his neck and face from the cold.

"I'm sorry to disturb you so late, but I need to speak with Mr. Hall," the man said.

"Well . . . I don't know . . ."

"It's very important."

Mother's shoulders slumped in resignation. "I'll tell him."

While he waited, the man hunkered down on one knee in front of Edie and pointed at the Christmas tree.

"I'll bet you made a lot of those lovely decorations," he said.

"Yes, I did," she replied, pleased that he had noticed.

His gaze went over the tree slowly and stopped when he saw the angel. She watched him studying the ornament.

"Do you believe in angels?" she asked shyly.

"Oh, yes, indeed!" he replied. "Don't you?"

"I don't know," she admitted honestly. "I wish I did, though. I'd like to meet one someday."

The man chuckled. "Maybe you have and just didn't recognize him," he suggested.

She turned and looked into his smiling eyes. "How would I know?" she asked.

His answer was interrupted by the sound of her father banging his fist on the table. "I don't care if he's the president himself!" he shouted. "Get rid of him!"

"Don't you worry, Edie," the man whispered as he stood up. "Angels always let you know. It's God's way of sending you a personal note of His love."

Mother returned, tight-lipped, drawing her shawl about her for comfort. Before she could speak, the stranger reached into his coat pocket and withdrew a plain white envelope.

"I'm sorry to have disturbed your family tonight," he said, handing her the envelope. "I just wanted to leave this with you, and tell Mr. Hall to report back to work at the mill tomorrow. He's got a new job there."

He winked at Edie. "Merry Christmas, Edie. And don't forget what I said: Angels always let you know."

It didn't occur to her to wonder how he knew her name.

"What a strange man," Mother murmured as she nervously tore the envelope open. The contents slipped through her trembling fingers and fluttered to the floor: three crisp $100 bills. For a long moment mother and daughter simply stared alternately at the money and at the door where the stranger had stood moments before.

Edie recovered first, scooped the three bills up, and handed them to her mother. Then they both ran toward the kitchen.

"Charley, you'll never believe what I have," Mother cried.

Startled by the strength in her voice, Charley's jaw dropped, and he stared at her in astonishment. Then he saw the money. "What's that?" he asked suspiciously, pointing at the bills.

"This is what the man at the door came to give you—along with some good news. You go back to work at the mill tomorrow," she said as tears filled her eyes. "I told you God would take care of us!"

Charley scrambled awkwardly out of his chair. "Where'd the man go? Call him back so I can talk to him."

"That's funny; I didn't hear his car leaving," Edie said before her mother could reply.

Bitterly cold air burst into the room when Charley opened the front door. He held the glass-topped kerosene lantern high over his head and looked out into the darkness.

"Hello!" he called. "Is anybody out there?"

Only a few snow flurries danced in the air.

"I don't see anything," the nearly blind man complained.

Edie pushed past her father. "Daddy, look at the ground," she whispered.

"What is it? What do you see?" he asked anxiously.

"Daddy, there are no footprints in the snow!"

Her father and mother slowly knelt beside her and examined the ground around them. Nearly eight inches of snow had accumulated that day. But the surface was smooth and undisturbed. Nobody had walked in that snow for hours.

"I just don't understand it!" Charley muttered over and over again.

Suddenly a broad, delighted smile spread over Edie's face. She looked at the angel on top of the Christmas tree and remembered the stranger's last words to her: "Angels always let you know!"

———

Epilogue: Shortly after the events described in this story, Charley Hall added another program to his favorite radio listening—the Voice of Prophecy. *A few months later he was baptized and joined his wife and children in attending the Seventh-day Adventist church in Auburn, Maine.*

21

That Hand

by Muriel Parfitt Polk

L et's show our moms we can climb the cliff," Lacey suggested to Erin.

The cliff must have been nearly 40 feet high. It was straight up and down, and covered with sharp, jagged rocks. Some of the rocks crumbled off easily and lay scattered around the base of the cliff.

Lacey, an active teenager, had scaled the cliff many times. Erin eagerly agreed to the suggestion. The girls started up the rocky cliff and easily made their way up to the top.

Lacey decided she wanted to go back down a more difficult and exciting way because the route up had been so easy. Looking around the cliff face, she pointed out another way down.

Erin looked it over. "Well, OK, I'll go that way if you go down first; then I'll follow."

Over the side Lacey went. Feeling with her hands and feet, she found fingerholds and toeholds. She slowly inched her way along as Erin watched from above. Lacey was only a short way down, reaching for another handhold, when the rock crumbled under her fingers. She lost her balance and began falling away from the cliff face.

Looking frantically around and below her, Lacey could see nothing to grab on to. There was nothing she could do. As she realized what was about to happen to her a thought flashed across her mind: *Will I be killed or crippled?*

Just then she felt something. A pressure in the small of her back pushed her toward the cliff. She grabbed the rocks tightly and glanced around. She could see that she was all alone. Erin was still on top, like a frozen white statue, her mouth open, gasping in alarm. Quickly Lacey climbed back up to the top, and she and Erin took the easier, safer way down.

Lacey often thought about the incident as she was growing up. She was puzzled about what had happened that day. When she was an adult she became a Christian. One day while she was reading the book *It Must Have Been an Angel** the memory of her experience on the cliff came back to her in sharp detail.

It was as if it were happening all over again—her beginning to fall, then that odd pressure on her back, the pressure in the shape of a large hand, the palm and five fingers each distinctly felt.

Lacey is sure she knows what it was that saved her that unforgettable day. "I can hardly wait to thank my guardian angel personally and shake that hand."

---

*Marjorie Lewis Lloyd, *It Must Have Been an Angel* (Mountain View, Calif.: Pacific Press Publishing Association, 1980).

22

The Three-Ton Miracle

by Lee Fross Cooper

I gazed out over the field, dotted with gray-green bales of fragrant alfalfa. Dad had cut the hay two days ago after work. Ed, my 13-year-old brother, had raked it into fat windrows the next afternoon. With the baler's work finished, I now drove the tractor in low gear, as Mother and Ed loaded the bales onto the long homemade sled.

Ten years before, when I was just a baby, Dad had built this "stoneboat" to haul rocks out of the fields. He had joined two 20-foot poles with two-foot-by-six-foot boards secured with spikes. Chains, threaded through holes in the large end of the logs, formed two loops. A thicker chain, always hanging from the tractor's drawbar, was hooked into these loops.

Now old and weathered, its crosspieces crumbling with rot, the stoneboat still made a great hay sled. It sure was a lot lower and easier than a tall hay wagon for Mother and Ed to heave the heavy bales into. Of course, since it didn't have wheels, it was more cumbersome to pull than a wagon would have been.

The sun beat down mercilessly as I guided the tractor between the rows. Rivulets of salty sweat trickled down to the corners of my mouth. I turned to check on the progress of the loaders. Bare to the waist, his suntanned back gleaming with perspiration, Ed seemed to be enjoying the work. My slender mother, as tan as we children, worked steadily in the stifling heat.

Approaching the end of the field, I had to make a wide turn to accommodate the long sled. The long rows of bales stretched ahead of me. The monotonous vibration of the tractor, combined with the shimmering heat, was almost lulling me to sleep.

Ed's voice shouting for me to stop jerked me back to my surroundings. I pushed in the clutch to halt the tractor and turned in my seat. Where were Ed and Mother? I couldn't see them.

"Alice, shut off the tractor," I heard Ed shout.

Quickly I turned the key, killing the engine. As I jumped to the ground, my body still tingled from the vibrations of the tractor.

Ed was kneeling on the ground. But where was Mother? It was as if she had vanished into thin air.

I thought I heard Ed say, "Shall I go for help?" I

ran across the uneven ground to where he knelt.

Oh, no! What I saw was so horrifying that I had never even imagined it. In an instant I saw that one of the rotting boards on the bed of the sled had broken when Mother had stepped up to fork a bale into place. Her leg had gone through the small hole and had been dragged under the sled, pulling the rest of her body onto the sled, her shoulder wedged tight against the big bales and her leg pinned beneath the sled. I started to cry.

Quietly Mother said, "Hush, Alice. Please don't fall apart now. I need you."

Ed repeated his question. "Should I go for help, Mother?"

"No," she answered. "All the men are in the fields. You children must help me. Jesus will give you the strength you need."

How could Mother be so calm? She told us to bow our heads while she asked Jesus to help us if it was His will. After her simple prayer, we all said amen together.

"Now, children," said Mother, "I want both of you to take a good firm hold of those poles, right out at the end. I'll count to three. When I say lift, lift the sled up so I can pull my leg out."

"Mother," cried Ed, "there are almost three tons of hay on this sled! We can't possibly lift it."

Mother's voice was firm. "If Jesus wants us to get this hay in the barn before tonight's rain, He will help you. If it is not His will, you will start unloading the hay. Let's let Him choose. Now get your hands around those poles!"

Mother counted, "One, two, three, *lift!*"

We lifted! And that load of hay went right up in the air! Mother pulled her leg up from under the sled. We lowered the stoneboat to the ground.

Ed and I looked at each other in amazement! How had we done that?

I could tell that Ed felt as shaky as I did. "The sled just jumped up in the air," he said in a quavery voice. Still unable to speak, I nodded my head in agreement.

Although it was skinned raw from ankle to hip, Mother's leg was not broken. We thanked Jesus for sending His angels to protect Mother from serious injury by helping two scared little kids lift three tons of hay.

23

Twister on the Tollway

by Don Dillon

B ye, Mom," I said as I grabbed my backpack from the back seat.

She kissed the top of my head. "Stay dry," she said. Angry-looking black clouds were rolling in.

"I will," I promised and headed up the front steps of Grandma's house. Mom worked the 3:00-11:00 shift at Mercy Hospital a couple days a week, and I stayed at Grandma's house until Dad got off work.

To my surprise, about a half hour later Mom was back. She looked pale and shaken. She picked up Grandma's phone and called the hospital, shutting the door so I couldn't hear what she was saying.

"Aren't you going to work today, Mom?" I asked after she'd hung up the phone.

"No," she said. "Come on, Donnie, we're going home."

What's going on? I wondered.

When we got home, Mom seemed really upset. She sat on the couch and just held me really close.

"What happened, Mom?" I asked.

"I just had a really bad scare. I'm OK, but I don't want to talk about it right now."

"OK." I went into the other room and turned on the TV.

Dad came home several hours later. Mom was talking in low tones in the kitchen. Dad never talks in low tones—I could hear him loud and clear.

"Oh, I don't think so," he said. "You probably just slipped and spun out on the wet pavement."

More mumbling.

"That's true," Dad said. "There's not enough room to spin out on the tollway ramp. It has those high concrete curbs."

Mumble, mumble.

"Well honey, you were badly frightened, but if it was a tornado, we would have heard about it on the news."

I flipped from my cartoons to the news station. The news had just started.

"A tornado touched down today on the Tristate Tollway . . ." the news anchor said.

"Dad, Mom, come see this!" I shouted.

A reporter was interviewing a tollbooth attendant. "Yes, it touched down right there on the ramp.

There was a little red Chevette coming up toward the tollbooth. The tornado picked up the car, and it went spinning through the air. Then it set it back down right on the ramp, except it was pointed in the opposite direction."

"Was the driver injured?"

"Apparently not. The Chevette sat there for a few minutes, and then moved slowly back down to the Stevenson Expressway. Then the owner drove off."

Is he talking about Mom? I wondered.

"Apparently there was no damage to the car either," the attendant continued.

"So it really was a tornado!" Mom said as she burst into tears. Dad just held her close. "It was so quiet!" she sobbed. "God was cupping my little car in His hands! All around me stuff was flying everywhere, but I was safe in His hands!"

Just that morning Mom had read to me a text from Isaiah. It said that nobody could pluck us out of God's hands. I walked over to the front door and peered out at the little red Chevette parked in our driveway. Then I went outside and walked around the car—twice. There was not a scratch.

I closed my eyes and said, "Thank you, Jesus, for taking care of my mom and for not letting the tornado pluck her out of Your hands."

24

Dreaming of Truth

by Roger Coon as told to Charles Mills

The old teacher was dying, and he knew it. But death didn't frighten him, because he understood what waited beyond that silent door. As he squinted into the warm Ethiopian sky, where hawks floated among the clouds, he thought to himself, *Yes, I understand, but so many others don't. That must be why God gave me the dream.*

"Send for my best students," he told the people who were caring for him. "Tell them to come here to Debre Tabor immediately. I have an important message to share with them."

In a matter of days his sickroom was jammed with sad-faced followers. They were trying to come to grips with the idea of living without their precious Sheh Zekarias, the man who'd spent most of his life traveling the dusty roads of Ethiopia introducing people to Jesus.

The teacher cleared his throat, and everyone became silent. "God has always called men and women to be instruments in His hands, willing to tell others about His love," he said.

Heads nodded in agreement as Zekarias rose up on one elbow. "God has shown me in a dream that He will send to you a group of people who will give you greater lights than what I've given you. Your minds will be impressed when you hear their message. It will be Bible-filled truth."

Then the old man said something very strange. "These people will baptize you by lowering you under the water. Their skin color will be different from yours, and when you meet them for the first time you'll hear them preaching one message in three different languages from the same pulpit."

The old man lay back on his pillow and closed his eyes. He died soon afterward.

Greater light? Baptizing under the water? Different skin color? What did all this mean? And how could a single message be preached in three languages from one pulpit?

Had Sheh Zekarias' illness made his thoughts confused? Was his dream nothing but the ramblings of an old man? These questions haunted his faithful followers as they returned to their villages.

But to one lifelong student of the great teacher, those dying words could be only one thing—a prophecy sent from God Himself.

Aleka Motbainor owned seven mules, four oxen, and many milking cows. This made him a well-to-do man in the town where he lived with his wife and three children.

However, Motbainor was restless. He, like many other devout Sheh Zekarias followers, had grown disgusted with their national religion.

"Saints and images, that's all they talk about," they complained among themselves. "Nowhere in the Bible does it say that we have to pray to saints or worship images."

Then Aleka Dessalign, a guest at Motbainor's home, told him about a faraway mission where people studied the Bible full-time.

"I will go to Asmara," Motbainor announced. "Sheh Zekarias said we should seek the truth, and that's what I am going to do."

A few days later he joined a group of traveling traders and embarked on the rough month-long journey. When he arrived at Asmara, in the country of Eritrea, just north of Ethiopia, who should he bump into but none other than his former houseguest, Aleka Dessalign.

The two friends hurried to meet a man named Dr. Albert Vener,* who offered Motbainor a room at his mission and made arrangements for his food. He even assigned a permanent Bible teacher to the grateful traveler.

After Motbainor had been with the mission for a few months, he was invited to attend a baptismal ceremony. To his surprise, the person for whom the ceremony was being held was a tiny baby. Before sprinkling water on the child, the pastor announced, "Now I baptize you, and later I will instruct you."

The visitor's mouth dropped open. How could this be? Any person being baptized must understand what's happening. Not only that, true baptism must be the same as what Jesus experienced in the Jordan River.

These are not the people I'm looking for, he told himself. *But where do I go from here?*

One Sunday morning Motbainor was sitting outside his house at the mission when he heard footsteps approaching. A stranger, noticing the open Bible in his lap, called out, "Sir, would you like to learn more about the Book you are reading?"

By this time Motbainor was so discouraged that he was ready for anything. "Yes," he replied with a tired smile.

"I'll be back next Saturday morning and take you to a place where all your questions will be answered. I'm Aleka Gebrat, from another mission here in Asmara," the stranger said warmly. "We hold services on Saturday, the Sabbath of the Bible. I'll pick you up then, OK?"

Six days later Gebrat arrived right on time and escorted the visitor to a small mud chapel set in a beautiful clearing surrounded by a grove of trees. Motbainor was all eyes and ears, drinking in everything he saw and heard.

When the main worship service began, he watched as a preacher walked to the big pulpit and started talking in English. Another man joined him on his left and translated his words into Swedish. Yet another gentleman rose and stood at his right, speaking to the assembly in Tigrinia, the local language.

Motbainor's breath caught in his throat. With his own eyes he was seeing a direct fulfillment of the prophecy given by his teacher and spiritual leader, Sheh Zekarias.

As the preacher spoke to his congregation that day, the lifework of a man he'd never met was reaffirmed in the mind of one of his listeners. At that moment Motbainor knew beyond a doubt that God was leading his search for truth.

"Where have you been?" Dr. Vener demanded when he returned to his house at the mission.

After hearing the response, the man frowned. "Those are Seventh-day Adventists! Keep away from them," he ordered flatly.

After three more months of living at the Swedish mission and worshiping with both groups, Motbainor felt he must terminate his host's hospitality and make new arrangements with his Adventist friends. They welcomed him with open arms and helped him continue his spiritual quest.

After much urging, the leader of the Adventist mission, V. E. Toppenberg, promised Motbainor that he'd train and send teachers and evangelists to the struggling Christians living in Ethiopia. The truth-seeker hurried home, eager to share the wonderful news that the dream had come true and that a wonderful new light would soon illuminate the darkest corners of their country.

Epilogue: Evangelists commissioned by the Adventist mission in Asmara did head south into Ethiopia, where they faced hardship and persecution. Again and again these dedicated men and women, along with their followers, were hurled into prison and persecuted; some were murdered. Motbainor's own home village was looted and burned twice. Gun-wielding vandals killed church elders and stole Adventist-owned livestock.

But the new believers pressed on. Some eventually stood before Ethiopian rulers, where, in a move that shocked the persecuting powers, God's people were finally given permission to preach Bible truth wherever the Holy Spirit led them.

---

* Not his real name

We've been curled.

Twirled.

Children can be so cruel.

Doodled on.

And telescoped.

Yet even when we feel persecuted, we know kids are learning about God, His goodness, and His grace. Our riveting stories, challenging puzzles, nature tales, and fun facts enthrall 10- to 14-year-olds with the gospel. Make sure your kids get their hands on *Guide* every week.

Guide. An invaluable resource for molding young minds. Even if it does get a little bent out of shape.

Now in Full Color!

See your Sabbath School secretary to order for your junior class. For home delivery, call **1-800-765-6955**.